Drew Provan

Mac Tips, Tricks & Shortcuts

in easy steps

covers OS X Mountain Lion
(OS X version 10.8)

In easy steps is an imprint of In Easy Steps Limited
4 Chapel Court · 42 Holly Walk · Leamington Spa
Warwickshire · United Kingdom · CV32 4YS
www.ineasysteps.com

Notice of Liability
Every effort has been made to ensure that this book contains accurate
and current information. However, In Easy Steps Limited and the
author shall not be liable for any loss or damage suffered by readers
as a result of any information contained herein.

Trademarks
OS X® is a registered trademark of Apple Computer, Inc. All other
trademarks are acknowledged as belonging to their respective
companies.

In Easy Steps Limited supports The Forest Stewardship Council (FSC),
the leading international forest certification organisation. All our titles
that are printed on Greenpeace approved FSC certified paper carry the
FSC logo.

MIX
Paper from
responsible sources
FSC
www.fsc.org FSC® C020837

Printed and bound in the United Kingdom

ISBN 978-1-84078-565-4

Contents

2 Essential Keyboard Shortcuts   71

3 Browsing the Net   81

4 Networking Tricks   91

9 Running Windows or Linux   145

10 Command Line Hacks   161

1 Finder Tips

The Finder is the control center for the Mac and you will spend much of your time using Finder windows. There are many ways in which you can adapt the Finder for your own needs.

10

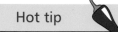

The Apple Menu gives you quick access to commonly-used functions, previously-opened documents and apps, and other utilities.

Using the Apple Menu

The Apple Menu is a great place to start exploring OS X. Click the Apple icon at the top left of the screen and a drop-down menu will appear. Using the Apple Menu you can:

1 Find out about your Mac's configuration

2 Check for Software Updates

3 Visit the App Store

4 View your System Preferences

5 Configure the Dock

6 View recent apps or documents

7 Force Quit apps

8 Put your Mac to sleep, restart, or shut down

9 Log out of your account

10 Holding down the **Shift** or **Option** keys gives you different options (*image below shows Apple Menu with Shift key pressed*)

| About This Mac |
| Software Update... |
| App Store... |
| System Preferences... |
| Dock ▶ |
| Recent Items ▶ |
| Force Quit Finder ⌥⇧⌘⏏ |
| Sleep |
| Restart... |
| Shut Down... |
| Log Out Drew Provan... ⇧⌘Q |

Dock options

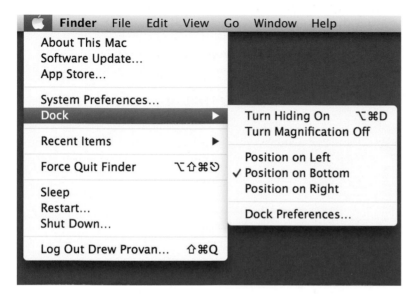

Recent Items

Resizing Window Columns

If you use the multiple column view (probably the most useful view) you often see document titles chopped off since they don't fit within the column.

You can manually drag the column by placing the pointer on the dividing line and moving the pointer to the right.

Quick, accurate column resizing

1 Place the pointer on the dividing line between two columns

2 Double-click

3 The column will now resize to the exact width that accommodates the longest document title

Before resizing a column

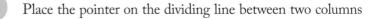

After double-clicking to resize

Change Finder Views

There are several Finder views. You can use the mouse to change views but keyboard shortcuts are much quicker! There are also keyboard shortcuts for many Finder options as shown in the table below.

A more comprehensive list of shortcuts is provided in Chapter Two.

Hot tip

Learn some basic keystrokes to help speed up your workflow.

Function	Keyboard shortcut
Finder Icon view	⌘ + 1
Finder List view	⌘ + 2
Finder Column view	⌘ + 3
Finder Cover Flow view	⌘ + 4
Show/Hide Toolbar	⌥ + ⌘ + T
Go Back	⌘ + [
Go Forward	⌘ +]
Show Enclosing folder	⌘ + up arrow
Show Computer	⇧ + ⌘ + C
Show Download folder	⌥ + ⌘ + L
Show Home	⇧ + ⌘ + H
Show Desktop	⇧ + ⌘ + D
Show Network	⇧ + ⌘ + K
Show Applications	⇧ + ⌘ + A
Show Utilities	⇧ + ⌘ + U
Go to folder	⇧ + ⌘ + G
Connect to Server	⌘ + K
Minimize window	⌘ + M
Cycle through windows	⌘ + `

⌘	Command key
⌥	Option (alt) key
⇧	Shift key

Finder Options

By default, OS X is not set up to show hard drives and other connected devices on the desktop (odd, since previous versions of OS X showed these). There are many adjustments to the Finder you can make and all are found at:

Finder > Preferences

Show connected drives

You can find settings for various types of drive under the **General** tab. You can also tell OS X how you want windows opened and also the Spring-loading delay time:

Use labels to highlight your files or folders

OS X provides color-coding if you look under the **Labels** tab. These are named according to color but you can change to anything you want to make it more useful. To use a color to highlight a file or folder simply right-click the item and choose the label you want to use.

Mac OS X's color-coding option for files and folders makes it really easy to find important files.

Default labels can be edited as shown on the image above

Fed up with being asked if you want to empty the Trash?

You can easily switch this off using the **Advanced** tab. Simply **uncheck** the *Show warning before emptying the Trash* then it won't ask you again!

Be warned, if you delete files they may be almost impossible to recover!

Control the Sidebar

The Sidebar contains your folders such as the Home folder, Applications, Movies etc. What you see, and the order they are shown, can be fully modified so you only see the items you want.

Customize the Sidebar
Under Finder Preferences choose the Sidebar tab and check or uncheck until you have the Sidebar customized to your needs.

Remove the Indicator Lights

These are the lights that show on the Dock to indicate which app is running (i.e. as opposed to being on the Dock but not active).

You can see Safari and Contacts are active in the image above but Apple Mail (in the center) is not.

Dock Options

You can switch off indicator lights and modify the Dock in many other ways by opening Dock Preferences:

Apple Menu > Dock > Dock Preferences

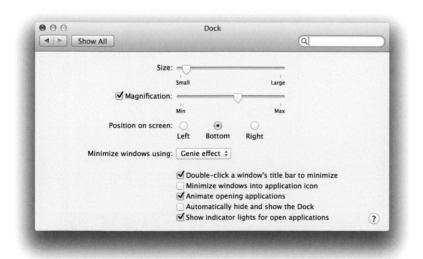

Resize Finder Icons

The icons you see on the Desktop and elsewhere may be perfect for your eyes, or you may prefer them to be larger or smaller. Achieving this is easily done using:

View > Show View Options (on the Menu Bar of the Finder)

Drag the slider right or left till you achieve the desired icon size.

You can also change the size of the text and the option to display the preview of the file (showing a preview can slow down older Macs and switching off the preview speeds things up).

Clean Up the Menu Bar

The Menu Bar is very useful since it holds items like the date and time, Wi-Fi, and many other functions. You can often determine what is shown on the Menu Bar from the Preference file for each item.

Hot tip

The items on the menu bar are not fixed — they can be moved around to suit your needs.

You can stop Date & Time showing on Menu Bar by unchecking the box at the top. The same can be done for Keyboard (below) and every other item that shows on the Menu bar.

Rearranging the order of items on the Menu Bar

Click an item while holding down the **Command** key and you can move items around the Menu Bar.

FTP using the Finder

Generally, file transfer (copying files to or from a server) is performed using an FTP (file transfer protocol) program such as Cyberduck (*http://cyberduck.ch*). But you can easily connect to servers from the Finder *without* using any software.

Connect to an FTP server

1 Press ⌘ + **K** to open a server search window

2 Enter the FTP details and press **Connect**

3 The FTP window will open like any regular Finder window and you can view files, upload and delete items easily

Customize Notification Alerts

Notifications in Mountain Lion are the same as those in iOS (iPhone, iPad, and iPod Touch). Essentially, apps can send you notifications of events, text messages, incoming emails, and many other types of activity on the Mac. How you see and hear these can be configured to suit your needs.

Go to **System Preferences > Notifications** to access the settings.

To see your notifications on the Mac click the icon at the top right of the screen (on a MacBook Pro you can see the notifications by sliding two fingers to the left on the trackpad).

Finding Files

Because Spotlight indexes your files based on their names and the data they contain, you can find any file you want fairly quickly. This powerful Spotlight indexing and search facility means that less filing of documents may be used, but in general it is still a good idea to create folders, much as you would do with a file cabinet rather than have all your documents in one folder.

There are several ways you can locate files.

Finder search window

1 Type ⌘ + **F**

2 A Finder search window opens

3 **Type the name of the file** *OR* some of the **text within the file** if you don't know the actual file name

4 The Finder will attempt to locate the file for you

In this example, I was trying to find a presentation about platelets that I had created within the last week: I typed ⌘ + **F** then typed *platelet* in the search box. Many files were found so I needed to narrow this down.

I changed *Kind* to *Presentation* which narrowed down the list but there were still too many files.

Hot tip

Keep adding criteria to the search to pinpoint the file you are looking for.

I added a *Created date* option and specified *within last 7 days* which reduced the list of files, showing the ones I was looking for.

Using Spotlight to Find Files

Instead of bringing up a Finder window, you can use Spotlight. There are two ways to access Spotlight:

 Click the Spotlight icon (magnifying glass at the top right of the screen)

 Or you can tap ⌘ + **Spacebar** which brings up the Spotlight search box

Hiding Sensitive Files

Later in the book we will look at ways of making encrypted disks to hold sensitive files. But here is a quick and easy way to create a folder which can be hidden and unhidden using the Terminal app.

To hide a folder called "mysecretfile"

1 Open Terminal and enter **chflags hidden ~/ Documents/mysecretfile**

2 The file is now hidden

Beware

If you intend to hide a file you must remember its name or you will never find it again!

To unhide

1 Enter **chflags nohidden ~/Documents/ mysecretfile**

25

Quick Look at Files

Sometimes, when you are looking through a group of files, you don't want the hassle of opening each and every one within a program. OS X lets you see the content of a file quickly using Quick Look. If it is the correct file, you can then double-click the file and open it using the appropriate app.

Using the Spacebar

Hot tip

Use Quick Look to see if a file is the one you want before opening it (will save you time).

1 Find the file and **click it once**

2 Tap the **spacebar** to open; tap again to close

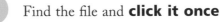

From File Menu

Select the file by clicking on it then go to **File > Quick Look**

Using keystroke

1 Click the file once

2 Press ⌘ + **Y**

Once you can view the file there are various things you can do, e.g. open in the appropriate program, preview (if it is an image), email it, Tweet it, and a few other actions.

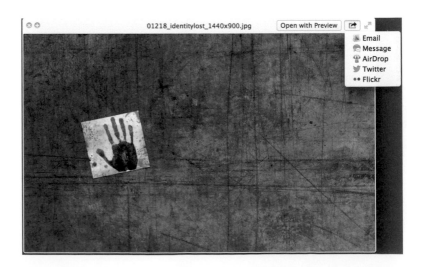

Keep Files in the Cloud

There's a lot of hype about cloud computing, but there are so many advantages to keeping files in the cloud that it makes sense to use a cloud to store much of your data.

In essence, the cloud is a remote server (usually multiple) on which you have some drive space. On the Mac you can often use the cloud as you would any other folder on your Mac, allowing you to drag-and-drop files into the cloud. So what? Well, if you have that cloud service running on your desktop and laptop, and perhaps an iPhone, iPad or other mobile device, you can see your cloud documents from any device! You no longer have to carry around USB drives to open your files on other devices.

iCloud is different

Apple's iCloud is a cloud service but there is no actual folder on your desktop and you cannot drag-and-drop.

Dropbox

This is a great cloud service. You can download the free app at *dropbox.com*. You then have a Dropbox folder on your Mac (or PC or pretty much all mobile devices). You get 2 GB free but you can buy more space if you need it.

Beware

You cannot drag-and-drop files into iCloud (unlike Dropbox and other services).

Dropbox

Opening Foreign Files

Sometimes you are sent files created by an app you don't have on your Mac. If you double-click the file, the Mac will tell you the program that created it cannot be found. But you can often still open the file and see the contents even if the layout is messed up.

For example, if someone gives me a QuarkXpress file I cannot see the content because I do not have QuarkXpress on my Mac. But I do have other apps that can open it which will give me a good idea of what the contents should look like.

I can also force the document into something like TextEdit and see the text but not the graphics and layout.

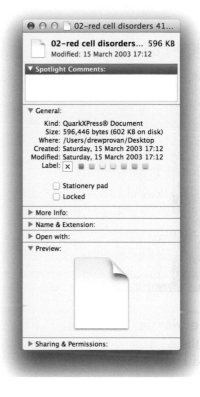

Opening with a similar program

1. **Right-click** the document

2. The Mac will suggest a program, in this case InDesign (similar to QuarkXpress). This will let me see the layout and probably the graphics too

3. But if I didn't have InDesign on my Mac, I could ask Microsoft Word, Pages, or TextEdit to try to open the file

4. At least within a word processing document I can grab the text I need and re-edit it

The Mac may suggest an appropriate app

In this case you can see my Mac has suggested InDesign.
But there are other options – simply click **Other...** and choose
different apps till you find one that opens the file.

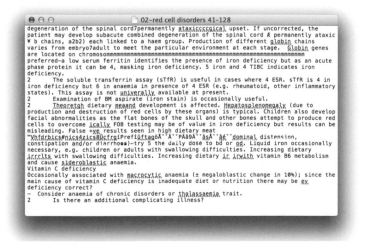

Viewing in TextEdit

Although the text doesn't look great, I can at least see the content
and I can edit either within TextEdit or copy and paste it into
Word or some other app. You can even see what the App Store
suggests (tap **App Store...**).

Hot tip

TextEdit is a great little text editor — it is fast, simple and good for making simple edits to text before placing in Word or Pages.

Viewing File Information

Sometimes you want to see how big a file is, its location, which app created it, and who has read/write permissions. This is easily done on the Mac using the File Information command: ⌘ + I. You can also click once on the file or folder and go to **File > Get Info**.

This document is 602 KB in size and is a QuarkXpress file. It is on the Desktop of my Mac. You can see the creation and modified dates. It is not locked (you can lock it from here by clicking the radio box). Sharing and permissions are hidden but clicking the triangle will show who can read and write to this file and these settings can be modified. You can tell this is a QuarkXpress document only because it says "Kind: QuarkXpress© Document". There is no QXP icon on the actual document.

This is a folder on my Mac (the Dropbox folder). It is 1.99 GB in size and it was created on 3 August, 2012 (the date I installed Dropbox).

It contains 1955 items (a mixture of files and folders). You can tell it's a folder because it states "Kind: Folder" and you can see the icon of the Dropbox folder at the bottom of the image.

File Sharing

Sometimes you need to share files with others. Previously, using OS X, you would need to send an email to someone and attach the file. Now, OS X makes it very easy to share documents with others, and also Tweet the file. You can also share image files with Facebook.

The options you see for sharing depend on the type of file you wish to share. If it is a picture, you have the option of sharing to Twitter, Flickr or Facebook (these are not available if the document is a text file).

Document sharing options
Here, a PowerPoint file has been right-clicked:

Sharing options with image files

Create Aliases

These are great time-savers! If there are folders you access regularly within your documents folder, make an alias and put it on the Desktop.

The alias points to the original file and if you drop anything onto the alias folder it gets added to the real folder. Similarly, if you delete anything from the alias it gets deleted from the real folder.

To make an alias of a folder

1 Locate the folder

2 Right-click and choose **Make Alias**

3 *Or* go to **File > Make Alias**

4 *Or* click once on the folder and type ⌘ **+ L**

Locate a Saved File

Sometimes you create documents but you cannot remember where you put them. There are several ways to find them.

Spotlight search

You can do a Spotlight search and refine the search to include all documents created within the last day.

If you know the program that you used to create the document, you can open that and look for Recent Files. If you can only remember some of the text within the document, then enter that into Spotlight.

I created a document which is important, but I saved as "*Imporrtant*" which means if I type "important" into Spotlight, the document will not be found.

If I then type only the first few characters "*impor*", then Spotlight will find it.

I can do a Finder search and not enter any name for the file but simply ask the Finder to show me all documents created within the last 0.05 days. My document now shows.

Alternatively I can open Pages (since I used this to create the document) and it will show me the recently-opened files which include the document I am looking for.

...cont'd

Using the Finder

Defining a specific type of file created within the last 0.05 days brings up today's file.

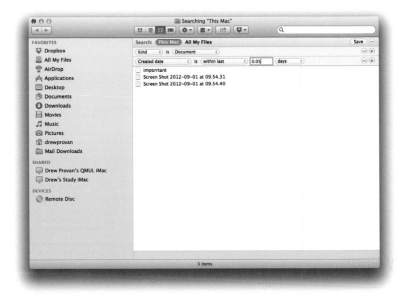

Using the app that created the document

Sort your Files using Finder

OS X provides many ways to sort your files. Most of us have them listed alphabetically (the default) but you can sort by: *Name, Kind, Application, Date Last Opened*, and several other ways.

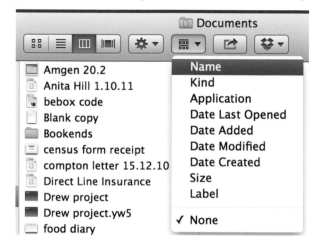

Here is my Documents folder, sorted using different methods:

By Kind

...cont'd

By Size

By Application

Create Folder from Selection

If you have a group of documents that you want to place into a folder, you could create the folder (⌘ + N) and then drop the files in. Or, the quick way is to lasso the files to select them all then right-click and choose **New Folder with Selection (n items)**.

Always Open With...

With files such as PDFs, JPEGs, TIFFs, etc. you can force the Mac to always open with one specific application rather than let OS X decide for you. For example, you may want PDFs to be opened only by *Adobe Acrobat* rather than *Preview*, or TIFF files only with *Adobe Photoshop* rather than *Preview*. By right-clicking on the file and holding down the Option key you can tell OS X to **Always Open With** a specific app. After that, every PDF will be opened only by Adobe Acrobat.

Hot tip

If you are tired of having to open files from within a program, tell the Mac to Always Open With... then it will remember to open that type of file with the app you have specified, rather than OS X's default setting.

38

The other way to achieve this is to go to **File > Open With** then hold down the Option key till you see **Always Open With**.

Basic Folder Housekeeping

Housekeeping is boring, as is folder housekeeping, but organizing your folders properly will save you lots of time later.

Numbered style
Numbering folders has two benefits: it brings them to the top of the list and it also lets you decide the order in which they are listed.

Occasionally, you want special folders to keep "to-do" items in. Start the title of the folder with a Z then it goes to the bottom of the list (you know it's there even though you may have to scroll down).

Putting a space or * before the folder title also forces it to the top of the list.

Color-coded
Use OS X's labeling feature to coordinate your folders into Personal, Work, Travel, Tax, etc.

Hot tip

Make any folder go to the top of the list by adding a space or * before the name. To make it go to the bottom add a Z before the title of the file or folder.

Let Smart Folders do the Work

OS X Smart Folders are special folders that automatically include any file within a specified set of criteria.

In the example below I wanted a folder that contains only presentations created in the last seven days.

Create Smart Folder

1. Go to **File > New Smart Folder**

2. Add criteria one at a time, e.g. **Kind is Presentation, Created date within the last 7 days**

3. The Smart Folder will be added to the Sidebar

4. Inside, you will see only those files you have specified. As the days go by, the files will change. If no new presentations are created over a week the folder will empty

New Finder Window	⌘N
New Folder	⇧⌘N
New Folder with Selection	^⌘N
New Smart Folder	⌥⌘N
New Burn Folder	
Open	⌘O
Open With	▶
Print	⌘P
Close Window	⌘W
Get Info	⌘I
Compress "pano2.jpg"	
Duplicate	⌘D
Make Alias	⌘L
Quick Look "pano2.jpg"	⌘Y
Show Original	⌘R
Add to Dock	⇧⌘T
Move to Trash	⌘⌫
Eject	⌘E
Burn "pano2.jpg" to Disc…	
Find	⌘F
Label:	

Name the Smart Folder

Here, you can give the Smart Folder any name you want and also specify the location where the folder is stored.

Look inside the Smart Folder

You will see the only files that fulfil these strict criteria.

Hide Running Apps

It is very easy to hide a running app. This is useful if you are on Facebook at work and the boss comes in!

Hiding an app quickly

 The app you want to hide needs to be active, i.e. it is not enough just to see the open app window; the app must be active (menu bars will not be gray)

 With the app active, press **Option + click anywhere on the Desktop**

Before Option + Click

After Option + Click

Launch Apps using Spotlight

To save time, rather than navigate your way to the Apps folder, you can launch apps directly from Spotlight.

Launch apps from Spotlight

1 Bring up the Spotlight search box by tapping ⌘ + **Spacebar**

2 Enter the first few characters of the app's name, e.g. "*Wo*" will bring up Microsoft Word

3 If Microsoft Word is highlighted, press **Enter**

4 If Microsoft Word is not highlighted, click on it then press **Enter**

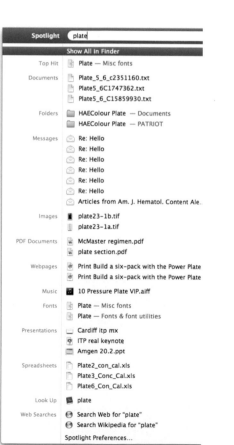

Streamline the Login Items

Each time you log in, certain apps and services are launched. The more items you have, the longer login takes and the more resources you use. It is a good idea to check your items from time to time and weed out any that you don't use:

1 Open **System Preferences > Users & Groups**

2 **Click the padlock** and authenticate to unlock in order to make changes

3 Click the **Login Items** button

4 Check through the list and remove those you don't need by pressing the "**-**"

Quick App Switching

You can switch between apps by clicking each app's icon on the Desktop or you can use the App Switcher feature.

Bring up App Switcher

1   Type ⌘ + **Tab**

2   The App Switcher showing running apps will appear

3   You can cycle through the apps by repeatedly hitting **Tab**

4   Quit an app by highlighting it, then hitting ⌘ + **Q**

5   Make an app active (come to the front) by selecting it, then clicking on its icon

Other actions while in App Switcher

- **tab** – move selection to the right in the app list
- **`** – move selection to the left
- **h** – hide the selected application
- **q** – quit the selected application
- **mouse scrollwheel** – move the selection back and forth
- **left arrow** – move selection to the left
- **right arrow** – move selection to the right

Gatekeeper Alerts

This security feature is built into OS X Mountain Lion and is there to protect you from installing rogue software. If the source is not recognized by your Mac, you will be prevented from running the installer for that app.

This can become irritating after a while and you can switch this feature off.

Configure Gatekeeper

1 Go to **Apple Menu > System Preferences > Security & Privacy**

2 Click the padlock and **authenticate** in order to make changes

3 At the bottom part of the window choose whether to allow software from **Anywhere** to be installed

4 Alternatively, you can choose only to allow installation from apps bought on the **Mac App Store**

Quick Hide/Show the Dock

If you have a huge screen you may not need to hide the Dock but if you are working on a smaller screen, hiding the Dock gives you a bit more screen real estate.

Hiding & Showing the Dock

1 Tap **Option + ⌘ + D** to hide the Dock

2 Tap **Option + ⌘ + D** to show it again

Before hiding Dock

After hiding Dock

Spotlight is a Calculator!

Slightly bizarrely, Spotlight can be used to perform calculations, saving you time since you don't need to open the calculator app.

Using Spotlight as a calculator

1 Open the Spotlight search box by tapping ⌘ + **Spacebar**

2 Enter your calculation

3 The result will be shown in the Spotlight search window

Spotlight	(24 + 9) * 2
	Show All in Finder
Calculator	66
Documents	AutoRecovery save of iPad draft contents...
	posting_body.tpl
	postgres_basic.sql
	overall_header.tpl
Messages	IK Krazy Deal – CSR at 78% Off!
	Interflora.co.uk – Order Confirmation: IN1...
PDF Documents	childhood ITP rituximab
	sardinian ITP genetic predisposition
	observational ITP study
	FCR in autoimmunity
	cytokines and autoimmunity
Webpages	30+ Super Secret OS X Features and Short...
	Ocado: Quality groceries that won't cost t...
Presentations	Amgen 20.2
	Amgen 20.2.ppt
	Amgen 20.2.12
	NPO–UKIRE–AMG–092–2011 Nplate RML_...
	Understanding_ITP_vs4.1_01_07_11_Spea...
Spreadsheets	Final v2 PBL Blizard Allocation to send to...
	Vendor set up form for Dr Drew Provan.xlsx
Web Searches	Search Web for "24 9 * 2"
	Search Wikipedia for "24 9 * 2"
	Spotlight Preferences...

Screenshots in Other Formats

On the Mac you can take screenshots using a variety of methods. The easiest is ⌘ + **Shift** + **3**. Other methods are detailed elsewhere in the book. The default image is a PNG file but you may prefer to have the image saved as a JPEG or TIFF. There are no system settings for this. Instead, you have to use Terminal and use a UNIX command to change the way OS X takes pictures of the screen.

Commands to change screenshot format

 Open Terminal

2 Type `defaults write com.apple. screencapture type jpg` if you want the screenshots saved as JPEG

3 If you want it saved as PDF type `defaults write com.apple.screencapture type pdf`

4 To change to TIFF enter `defaults write com. apple.screencapture type tiff`

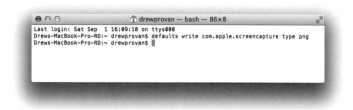

Taking different types of screenshot

Full screen: (Save to Desktop) – ⌘ + **Shift** + **3**

Full screen (Save to Clipboard) – ⌘ + **CTRL** + **Shift** + **3**

Select region (Save to Desktop) – ⌘ + **Shift** + **4**

Select region (Save to Clipboard) – ⌘ + **CTRL** + **Shift** + **4**

Select item (Save to Desktop) – ⌘ + **Shift** + **4 then Spacebar**

Select item (Save to Clipboard) – ⌘ + **CTRL** + **Shift** + **4 then Spacebar**

Editing Screenshots

The easiest way to edit screenshots is in Preview. If you double-click a screenshot, Preview will open (unless you have told the Mac to open PNG files in another app).

Once open, you can crop, rotate, annotate, and more from within Preview.

You can see some of the editing tools available in Preview below.

I have added an arrow and thought-bubble to this image.

Create an Encrypted USB Drive

If you have sensitive files and want to hide them, you can buy an encrypted USB drive but they can be expensive. You can easily make one yourself using a standard USB drive.

Make an encrypted USB dive

 Open Disk Utility

 Click the **Erase** tab

③ Choose **Mac OS Extended (Journaled, Encrypted)**

...cont'd

 Name the USB drive

 Enter the **password** you want to use

 Add a **hint** if necessary

 Do *not* add to Keychain otherwise the drive will open automatically when you insert it into your Mac (the whole object is to have it password protected!)

 Now, when you insert the USB drive you will need to enter the password in order to access the drive

Reveal your own Library

Since OS X Lion, the User Library has been hidden by default (oddly, the Main Library remains visible, however). The User Library contains the Preference files for the apps you use.

Temporarily show User Library

 On the Menu Bar select **Go** then press **Option**

2 After pressing Option, the User Library is visible. Click it to open it

Permanently Show User Library

1 Open **Terminal**

2 Type **chflags nohidden /Users/username/ Library** where username is the name of your Home Folder

3 Your library will now appear and will remain visible

Running Multiple Desktops

If you want to run several apps simultaneously, the Desktop can become crowded, with the windows of the various apps overlapping. It is much easier to assign a separate Desktop to each app and flick backwards and forwards between them.

Mission Control in Mountain Lion allows you to make several Desktops as you need them. In the Mission Control window you can place apps into separate Desktops.

Assigning apps to Desktops

54

1 **Launch Mission Control** (from the Dock or double-tap the mouse or keypad)

2 **Drag apps** to separate Desktops

3 **Make new Desktops** by clicking the icon at the top right of the screen (a **+** symbol will appear)

4 Toggle between the various Desktops by tapping **Control + right or left arrow**

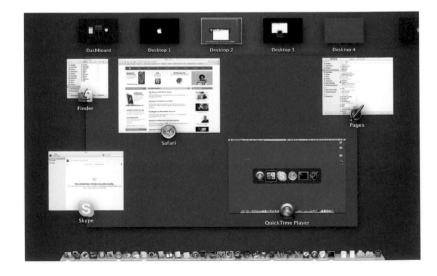

Switch Resume On/Off

Shutting down the Mac used to involve quitting all apps and the need to save all your work. Now you can shut down your Mac and it will remember which apps you had open and reopen these when you restart (even if you do a full shutdown).

In Lion (OS X 10.7) there was an option in General System Preferences to always Resume but that option has been removed with OS X 10.8 and the Resume function appears only when you tell the Mac to shut down.

If you want all apps to reopen on restart

If you do NOT want all apps to reopen on restart

Hide Unwanted System Prefs

The System Preferences give you control over many aspects of your Mac. By default, all preferences are displayed when you open the app. You can, however, choose to hide certain preference panes by editing the window:

1 Go to **System Preferences > View > Customize**

2 **Uncheck** the preferences you want to hide

Mountain Lion Tweaks

You can modify OS X on your Mac piecemeal using Terminal commands and other options hidden within various apps but there is a freeware app that lets you change a ton of features.

Mountain Tweaks

Go to *tweaksapp.com/app/mountain-tweaks/* and download the app. Drag it to your Applications folder and run the app from there. Be careful what you change in case your Mac starts behaving oddly. If all goes wrong, you can always click the Restore button and your Mac will be back to where it was before you started tweaking it.

General Tweaks

These let you change features common to both Lion and Mountain Lion.

Hidden Second Clipboard

The Mac only has one clipboard. When you select Copy (⌘ + C) the information is sent to the Clipboard. If you copy again, the original clipping is lost. Within certain apps, e.g. TextEdit, you can use a hidden second clipboard by using certain commands:

Kill: Ctrl + K

Yank: Ctrl + Y

With text selected, **Ctrl + K** works as a secondary "cut" command by removing the highlighted text without replacing what is currently residing in your clipboard.

To bring the text back, use **Ctrl + Y**.

Kill has other uses
"Kill" has other uses apart from the "cut" command. If you place your cursor at a given point in a paragraph and hit Ctrl + K, all of the text from that point forward will be cut. This is a useful way to quickly grab and move an entire paragraph of text.

Disadvantages
Ctrl + K only works on editable text (e.g. TextEdit and Mail). You can't "kill" text on a web page.

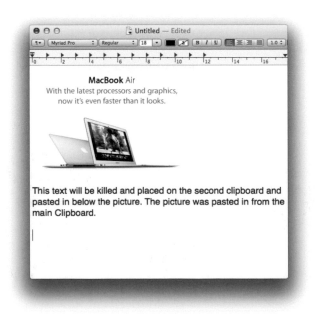

Accessing Emoticons

If you like using emoticons (picture images that act like text characters) you can find these easily from the Character Viewer.

Show Character Viewer

 Open **System Preferences** and click on **Keyboard**

 Make sure **Show Keyboard & Character Viewers** in the Menu Bar is checked

You will then see the Keyboard & Character Viewer icon in the Menu Bar

Click to show **Character Viewer**

Choose the option you want (People, Nature, etc), find the character you want to use in your document and double-click it. It will then be placed into the document

Mouse & Trackpad

When you click, double-click, or triple-click the trackpad, you have to physically click the trackpad by default, depressing the trackpad in order for the Mac to register the click. It is much easier to allow **Tap to Click** so that gently tapping the surface of the trackpad registers as a click.

Configure Tap to Click

 Go to **Apple Menu > System Preferences > Trackpad**

 Check the top option **Tap to Click**

Speed up your mouse!
Some people (me included) are speed freaks and like their mouse pointer to zoom across the screen at high speed.

Speeding up the mouse is easy.

Speed up your mouse

① Go to **Apple Menu > System Preferences > Mouse**

② Check the top option **Tap to Click**

 Drag the Tracking slider right or left until you find the speed that suits your needs best

Access the Dictionary

OS X has an inbuilt dictionary that can be invoked from within any app.

To access the Dictionary

 Double-click the word you wish to look up

Hot tip

You can bring up the Dictionary from within any app.

2 Once highlighted, **right-click and choose Look Up**

3 The definition and pronunciation will be shown

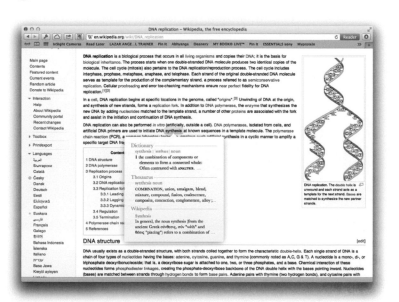

Deactivate Widgets

Widgets are small apps that run continuously, showing you the weather, stocks and shares and other information. They can be found on the screen to the left of the main screen (press **Control + left arrow** to see or use Mission Control).

There are thousands of widgets you can install but these use RAM and can slow your Mac down. In general it is best not to have too many of these running at any one time.

Deactivating is easy

1 Go to the widget screen (Control + ←)

2 Click the ⊖ symbol and you will see ⊗ appear on each widget

3 Tap ⊗ for every widget you wish to remove

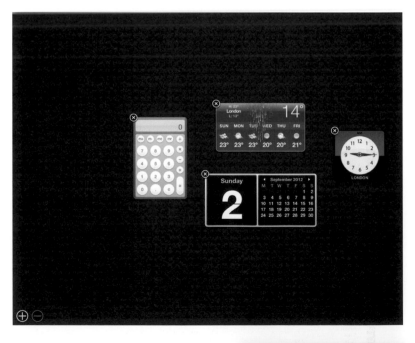

Add more widgets by clicking the (**+**) symbol.

Save Text as Snippets

You can drag pieces of text from documents onto the desktop and use these later by dropping them onto a word processing document or other types of document. This gets round the limited number of clipboards provided by OS X. You could keep several small pieces of text, all dragged from a website or other document, and drop these one-by-one onto a new document.

To make a Snippet

1 **Select the text** you want to save as a Snippet

2 **Drag the highlighted text** to the Desktop or folder

3 When you want to use the text Snippets, drag onto a new document

Drop the Snippet onto a new document

You can then tidy up the text, reformat, etc.

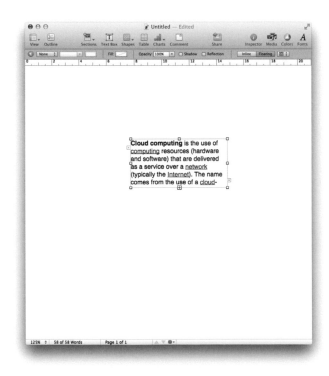

Using System Information

The **About This Mac** app under the Apple Menu provides a lot of information about your Mac.

Launch System Information

1 Go to **Apple Menu > About This Mac**

2 Click **More Info...**

3 Cycle through the tabs to see the full specs of your Mac, including RAM upgrade options

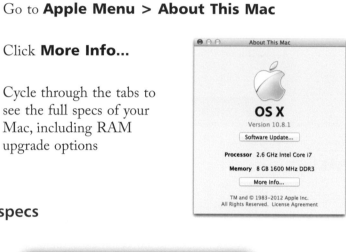

Basic specs

Screen resolution

...cont'd

Storage

RAM

Service options

Clean Install of OS X from USB

OS X is purchased from the App Store, and after installation the installer is *deleted* from your Applications folder. In order to get OS X onto a USB stick you need to download OS X *but not install* until you have made a copy of the installer!

Creating the OS X Mountain Lion on USB stick

1 **Locate the Install OS X Mountain Lion** installer in the Applications folder

2 **Right-click** to Show Package Contents

Beware

If you download and install Mountain Lion, the installer is removed from your Applications folder.

67

3 **Double-click** to show package contents

4 **Double-click** the SharedSupport folder

...cont'd

 Right-click InstallESD.dmg file

6 Select **Disk Utility** from the **Open With** menu

 Select your USB drive from the list on the left and click the Partition tab

8   Set the Partition to **1 Partition**, set the name to
    MOUNTAINLION, set the format to **Mac OS
    Extended (Journaled)** and then click the **Options**
    button

9   Choose **GUID partition table** and click **OK**

...cont'd

10 Click **Apply** to save changes

11 When asked to confirm, **click** the Partition button

12 **Right-click the InstallESD.dmg image** from the left side of Disk Utility and choose **Open Disk Image** from the popup

13 **Select** the new Mac OS X ESD partition then click **Restore**

14 Ensure Max OS X Install ESD is set as the Source and then **drag** MOUNTAINLION partition from the list on the left to the Destination field

15 Click the **Restore** button then click Erase to begin the install

16 Log in and enter the administrator **password**

17 When the restore is complete, the USB drive will mount and is ready to use

2 Essential Keyboard Shortcuts

In the days before the mouse, computer users relied entirely on keyboard commands. Today we tend to control our Macs using the mouse but you can speed up your workflow hugely if you use keystrokes for common actions.

This chapter lists most of the keystrokes you are ever likely to need. Spend time and learn some basic ones and you will stop relying on the mouse for common tasks.

Finder and other Shortcuts

Everyone should know a few shortcuts, even if it's just the basic cut-and-paste shortcuts. They can speed up your workflow considerably, so try to memorize and use these basic shortcuts before moving on to the more advanced ones.

If you're coming from a Windows environment you may be used to Control + C, Control + V etc. For any Windows shortcut, simply substitute Control for Command (⌘) on the Mac and the chances are the shortcut will work!

The Basic Shortcuts	
Copy (text, image, etc)	⌘ + C
Paste	⌘ + V
Cut (delete)	⌘ + X
Undo last action	⌘ + Z
Print	⌘ + P
Open doc, folder, etc.	⌘ + O
Save	⌘ + S
Save as	Option + ⌘ + S
Repeat an action	⌘ + Y
Select all	⌘ + A

Finder Shortcuts	
Accessibility Options	⌘ + Option + F5
Add Selected Item to Sidebar	⌘ + T
Close All Windows	⌘ + Option + W
Close Window	⌘ + W
Connect to server	⌘ + K
Copy Item	⌘ + C
Cut	⌘ + X
Dashboard	F12 (fn + F12 on laptops)
Dictation	Tap Function key twice
Display the Restart/Sleep/Shut Down confirmation dialog box	Control + Eject
Duplicate	⌘ + D
Eject selected volume	⌘ + E
Empty Trash	⌘ + Shift + Delete

Find	⌘ + F
Force Empty Trash	⌘ + Shift + Option + Delete
Force Quit	⌘ + Option + escape
Get Info	⌘ + I
Go Back	⌘ + [
Go Forward	⌘ +]
Go to All My Files	⌘ + Shift + F
Go to Applications Folder	⌘ + Shift + A
Go to Computer Folder	⌘ + Shift + C
Go to Desktop	⌘ + Shift + D
Go to Enclosing Folder	⌘ + ⎵
Go to Folder	⌘ + Shift + G
Go to Home Folder	⌘ + Shift + H
Go to Network Folder	⌘ + Shift + K
Go to Utilities Folder	⌘ + Shift + U
Help	⌘ + Shift + ?
Hide Current Application	⌘ + H
Hide Finder	⌘ + H
Hide Toolbar	⌘ + Option + T
Log Out (with confirmation)	⌘ + Shift + Q
Log Out (without confirmation)	⌘ + Option + Shift + Q
Log Out Current User	⌘ + Shift + Q
Mac Help	⌘ + ?
Make Alias	⌘ + L
Minimize All	⌘ + Option + M
Minimize Window	⌘ + M
Mission Control: All Windows	Control + ⌘ (F3 on Apple keyboards)
Mission Control: Show Desktop	F11 (fn + F11 on laptops) (⎵ + F3 on Apple keyboards)
Move to Trash	⌘ + Delete
New Finder Window	⌘ + N
New Folder	⌘ + Shift + N
New Smart Folder	⌘ + Option + N
Next Window	⌘ + `

...cont'd

Open	⌘ + O
Open Applications folder	⌘ + Shift + A
Open Computer folder	⌘ + Shift + C
Open enclosing folder	⌘ + ⊡
Open Inspector	⌘ + Option + I
Paste	⌘ + V
Power options dialog	Control + Eject
Preferences	⌘ + ,
Quick Look	⌘ + Y or spacebar or tap trackpad 3 times
Restart	⌘ + Control + Eject
Restart (without confirmation, but you can save changes in open documents)	⌘ + Control + Eject
Save As	Hold down Option in Find menu
Select All	⌘ + A
Show Inspector	⌘ + Option + I
Show Original (of selected alias)	⌘ + R
Show View Options	⌘ + J
Show/Hide Dock	⌘ + Option + D
Show/Hide Sidebar	⌘ + Option + S
Show/Hide Status Bar	⌘ + /
Shut Down (without confirmation, but you can save changes in open documents)	⌘ + Control + Option + Eject
Sleep	⌘ + Option + Eject
Sleep (without confirmation)	⌘ + Option + Eject
Sleep display	Shift + Control + Eject
Spotlight menu	⌘ + spacebar
Spotlight window	⌘ + Option + spacebar
Turn VoiceOver On/Off	⌘ + F5 (fn + F5 on laptops)
Turn Zoom On/Off	⌘ + Option + 8
Undo	⌘ + Z
View Window as Columns	⌘ + 3
View Window as Cover Flow	⌘ + 4

View Window as Icons	⌘ + 1
View Window as List	⌘ + 2

Text Editing

Go to the start/end of the line	⌘ + ← / ⌘ + →
Go to the start/end of the document	⌘ + ↑ / ⌘ ↓
Go to the previous/next word	Option ← / Option →
Go to the previous/next paragraph	Option ↑ / Option ↓
With selection: web search/ sticky note	⌘ + Shift + L / ⌘ + Shift + Y
Cut/Copy/Paste	⌘ + X / ⌘ + C / ⌘ + V
Select All	⌘ + A

Mission Control

View Mission Control	Control + ↑
Show app's windows	Control + ↓
Show desktop	F11
Show Dashboard	F12
Move between Desktops	Control + ← / Control + →
Show windows for next app after Control ↑	Tab
Enlarge window under cursor after Control ↑	Spacebar
Switching apps and windows	
Advance to next app	⌘ + Tab
Next window in current app	⌘ + `
Hide/Show Dock	⌘ + Option + D

Accessibility Controls

Toggle zoom feature (turn on to use zoom)	⌘ + Option + 8
Zoom in/out (also Control and mouse scroll)	Option + ⌘ + =/Option + ⌘ + -
Show Accessibility Controls	⌘ + Option + F5

...cont'd

Application Commands

New window	⌘ + N
App preferences	⌘ + ,
Open file	⌘ + O
Hide app	⌘ + H
Close window	⌘ + W
Hide others	⌘ + Option + H
Save	⌘ + S
Save As	⌘ + Shift + S
Show fonts panel	⌘ + T
Show colors panel	⌘ + Shift + C
Print	⌘ + P
Quit	⌘ + Q
Full Screen Mode	⌘ + Control + F
Help	⌘ + Shift + /

Safari Shortcuts

Preferences	⌘ + ,
Block Pop-Up Windows	⌘ + Shift + K
Empty Cache	⌘ + Option + E
New Window	⌘ + N
New Tab	⌘ + T
Open File	⌘ + O
Open Location	⌘ + L
Close Window	⌘ + W
Close All Windows	⌘ + Option + W
Save As	⌘ + S
Mail Contents of This Page	⌘ + I
Mail Link to This Page	⌘ + Shift + I
AutoFill Form	⌘ + Shift + A
Show/Hide Bookmarks Bar	⌘ + Shift + B
Show/Hide Tab Bar	⌘ + Shift + T
Show/Hide Status Bar	⌘ + /
Show/Hide Reader	Shift + Option + R

Show/Hide Reading List	Shift + Option + L
Stop	⌘ + .
Reload Page	⌘ + R
Make Text Normal Size	⌘ + 0
Make Text Bigger	⌘ + +
Make Text Smaller	⌘ + −
View Source	⌘ + Option + U
Back	⌘ + [
Forward	⌘ +]
Home	⌘ + Shift + H
Search Results SnapBack	⌘ + Option + S
Show All Bookmarks	⌘ + Option + B
Add Bookmark	⌘ + D
Add Bookmark Folder	⌘ + Shift + N
Add to Reading List	⌘ + Shift + D
Select Previous Item in Reading List	⌘ + Option + Up arrow
Select Next Item in Reading List	⌘ + Option + Down arrow
Select Previous Tab	⌘ + Shift + Tab
Select Next Tab	⌘ + Tab
Downloads	⌘ + Option + L
Activity	⌘ + Option + A
Safari Help	⌘ + ?

Apple Mail Shortcuts

Attach File	⌘ + Shift + A
New Message	⌘ + N
New Note	⌘ + Control + N
Open Message	⌘ + O
New Viewer Window	⌘ + Option + N
Save As	⌘ + Shift + S
Save	⌘ + S
Append Selected Messages	⌘ + Option + I
Find	⌘ + F
Find Next	⌘ + G

...cont'd

Find Previous	⌘ + Shift + G
Paste as Quotation	⌘ + Shift + V
Paste and Match Style	⌘ + Option + Shift + V
Show Spelling and Grammar	⌘ + :
Check Spelling	⌘ + ;
Jump to Selection	⌘ + J
Use Selection for Find	⌘ + E
Mailbox Search	⌘ + Option + F
Reply-To Address Field	⌘ + Option + R
Bcc Address Field	⌘ + Option + B
Show/Hide Deleted Messages	⌘ + L
Hide/Show Mailbox List	⌘ + Shift + M
All Headers	⌘ + Shift + H
Raw Source	⌘ + Option + U
Plain Text Alternative	⌘ + Option + P
Select All Messages in This Conversation	⌘ + Shift + K
Erase Deleted Items	⌘ + Shift + Delete
Erase Junk Mail	⌘ + Option + J
Get All New Mail	⌘ + Shift + N
Go to Inbox	⌘ + 1
Go to Outbox	⌘ + 2
Go to Drafts	⌘ + 3
Flag (red)	⌘ + Shift + L
Mark as Junk Mail	⌘ + Shift + J
Mark as Unread/Mark as Read	⌘ + Shift + U
Add Sender to Address Book	⌘ + Shift + Y
Apply Rules	⌘ + Option + L
Reply	⌘ + R
Reply All	⌘ + Shift + R
Forward	⌘ + Shift + F
Redirect	⌘ + Shift + E
Reply with iChat	⌘ + Shift + I
Send Again	⌘ + Shift + D
Bigger	⌘ + +

Smaller	⌘ + -
Copy Style	⌘ + Option + C
Show Colors	⌘ + Shift + C
Show Fonts	⌘ + T
Increase Quote Level	⌘ + '
Decrease Quote Level	⌘ + Option + '
Make Rich/Plain Text	⌘ + Shift + T
Address Panel	⌘ + Option + A

Startup Keys

Choose boot volume	Option
Reset PRAM	⌘ + Option + PR
Single user mode boot	⌘ + S
Disk Utility and Internet recovery	⌘ + R
Go into Target disk mode	T

Dock Shortcuts

Turn hiding off or on	⌘ + Option + D
Move to the next open application	⌘ + Tab
Move to the previous open application	⌘ + Shift + Tab
Minimize a window	⌘ + M
Highlight/unhighlight the Dock	Control + F3
Move among Dock items when it is highlighted	Left/right arrow keys

Screenshots

Take a screenshot of the screen, and save it as a file on the desktop	⌘ + Shift + 3
Take a screenshot of an area and save it as a file on the desktop	⌘ + Shift + 4, then select an area
Take a screenshot of a window and save it as a file on the desktop	⌘ + Shift + 4, then space, then click a window

...cont'd

Take a screenshot of the screen, and save it to the clipboard	⌘ + Control + Shift + 3
Take a screenshot of an area and save it to the clipboard	⌘ + Control + Shift + 4, then select an area
Take a screenshot of a window and save it to the clipboard	⌘ + Control + Shift + 4, then space, then click a window

Startup Key Combinations

Start up from a bootable CD, DVD, or USB thumb drive (such as OS X install media)	Press C during startup
Start up in Apple Hardware Test (AHT)	Press D during startup
Reset NVRAM	Press Option + ⌘ + P + R until you hear startup sound a second time.
Start up in Startup Manager, where you can select an OS X volume to start from. Note: Press N to make the first bootable Network volume appear as well.	Press Option during startup
Ejects any removable media, such as an optical disc.	Press Eject, F12, or hold the mouse or trackpad button
Attempt to start up from a compatible network server (NetBoot)	Press N during startup
Start up in Target Disk Mode	Press T during startup
Start up in Safe Boot mode and temporarily disable login items	Press Shift during startup
Start up in Verbose mode	Press ⌘ + V during startup
Start up in Single-User mode	Press ⌘ + S during startup
Start from a NetBoot server using the default boot image	Press Option + N during startup
Start from Recovery partition	Press ⌘ + R during startup

3 Browsing the Net

Safari is a great browser and you can

adapt it to your own needs very easily.

Change your Default Browser

Safari is the default browser in OS X. This is not surprising since it is the only browser installed with OS X and it is Apple's own. However, you may have installed Google Chrome, Firefox, or another browser, yet every time you click a web link Safari opens!

How to choose another default browser

1 Open Safari and go to **Preferences > General**

2 In the dropdown menu, set the **Default web browser:** to whatever you want (*only those browsers you have installed will show up in the list*)

Sharing web pages

There are several ways in which you can share web pages. The latest version of Safari allows you to:

- Add to reading list

- Add bookmark

- Email this page

- Message

- Twitter

- Facebook

You can find these options on the toolbar to the left of the main address bar. The icon is an arrow pointing up and to the right.

Select another Search Engine

Google is the search engine installed with Safari. You may wish to change this to Bing or Yahoo! and this is very straightforward.

Changing the default search engine

1 **Open Safari**

2 Go to **Preferences > General**

3 Look for **Default search engine:** and you will see Google is the default option

4 Click Google and a drop-down menu will show Yahoo! and Bing

5 Choose the engine you wish to use and, from now on, any searches you do will be carried out using your chosen search engine

Save Web Pages for Later

Quite often you will look at a number of websites but not have time to read the entire content at each site. It is very easy, using the reading lists, to add websites for off-line reading later.

Adding a web page to the reading list

1 **Open Safari**

2 Navigate to the web page you wish to save

3 Go to **Bookmarks > Add to Reading List**

4 Alternatively, press **Shift + ⌘ + D**

5 The web page will be added to the Reading List (found on the main Safari web page on the extreme left of the toolbar)

Show All Bookmarks	⌥⌘B
Add Bookmark...	⌘D
Add Bookmarks for These Tabs...	
Add Bookmark Folder	⇧⌘N
Add to Reading List	⇧⌘D
Add These Tabs to Reading List	
Select Previous Item in Reading List	⌥⌘↑
Select Next Item in Reading List	⌥⌘↓
📖 Bookmarks Bar	▶
📁 BT Total Broadband	▶
📁 Broadband speed testers, IP addresses	▶
📁 Consumables – toner, pool chemicals, stationery	▶
📁 Drew new Wordpress site	▶
📁 Drew personal	▶
📁 Finance	▶
📁 Fonts	▶
📁 Fraser	▶
📁 General Geek Stuff	▶
📁 Guitar stuff	▶
📁 iPhone	▶
📁 Presentation stuff	▶
📁 QMUL	▶
📁 Rapidweaver, forum, registry	▶
📁 Webspace providers	▶
📁 ITP	▶
📁 Frequent flyer	▶

Reset Safari

After you have been using Safari for a while, you will collect cookies, images and other temporary items whilst browsing many websites, which will be stored in your User Library. You may also have filled in online forms and generated passwords for websites which you will obviously want to keep. However, it is a good idea to reset Safari from time to time to clear out all of these unwanted files, but leave the autofill and password data.

Resetting Safari

1. **Open Safari**

2. Go to **Safari > Reset Safari...**

3. The Reset Safari window will open, showing a number of options including one to clear history, reset top sites, remove all web page preview images, reset all location warnings, reset all website notification warnings, remove all website data, and others. I recommend checking all of these *except* **Remove saved names and passwords**, and **Remove other AutoFill form text**

4. **Press Reset**

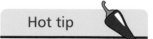

Hot tip

Reset Safari (or any browser you use regularly) to stay secure.

85

Get rid of Cookies!

Cookies are small pieces of data sent by websites to your browser where they are stored. Cookies provide useful information to companies about your browsing habits, shopping habits and other information. Cookies allow web pages to show you adverts likely to be of interest to you based on your past browsing history. Some people feel that cookies are intrusive and many people block cookies at all times.

Modern browsers have an option to block cookies and you may wish to activate this in Safari. Some websites will not allow you to browse the site unless you accept a cookie. In general, it is a good idea to remove cookies from time to time.

Removing cookies from Safari

1 **Open Safari**

2 Go to **Preferences > Privacy**

3 Click the button **Remove All Website Data...** next to Cookies and other website data:

You also have the option within this window to block cookies **From third parties and advertisers**, **Always**, or **Never**. You also have the option to ask websites not to track you.

Using Safari Tabs

Having tabs in Safari is very useful because you can open 10 or more individual websites, and if you activate tabbed browsing, you can have all of these websites active and running, each within its own tab, along your tab bar underneath the toolbar.

Before tabbed browsing became possible you had to live with multiple web pages being open on your screen, stacked on top of each other, which made navigation very difficult.

Tabbed browsing is much more elegant, and in Mountain Lion there is even an option to show all the tabbed web pages side-by-side.

Create a new tab in Safari

1. With Safari open, click ⌘ + **T** and a new tab will be placed to the right of the initial tab

2. If you press ⌘ + **T** again, a third tab will appear to the right of the tab you just created

3. If you tap the icon to the extreme right of the tab bar, you will see your tabs side-by-side in a scrolling window which you can navigate, right and left, using two fingers on the trackpad

Organize your Bookmarks!

Over time, you will collect many bookmarks in Safari. If you are organized, you will create categorized folders to store your bookmarks in their respective categories. If you do not create folders you will simply have a long list of bookmarks and it will be impossible to find anything!

Unfortunately, Safari does not make it easy to sort your bookmarks, since there is no way of making your bookmarks alphabetical, although there are third-party apps which will do this for you. So, unless you use one of these apps, you will be forced to sort the lists manually.

Managing your Bookmarks

 **Beware**

There is no alphabetical sort facility in Safari. You will need to use a third-party app such as Bookdog.

1 Open Safari and click **Bookmarks**

2 Click **Show Bookmarks**

A complete list of your bookmarks will appear, showing various folders, with all unfiled bookmarks at the bottom of the screen. From here, you can delete and file the bookmarks.

Search Google in any App

Google is a useful search engine for Safari or any other browser. With Mountain Lion you can search Google within any application, e.g. a browser, word processor, and many other types of app.

Searching Google within a word processor

1 Open the word processor and **double-click the text** you wish to search

2 **Right-click** the selected text

3 Go to the bottom of the drop-down menu and choose **Search in Google**

4 You will then be taken to Safari, or your preferred browser, and Google will have searched for the words you highlighted

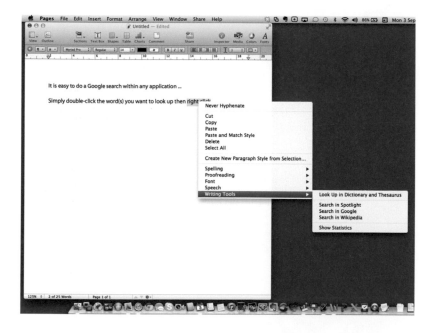

Download YouTube Videos

YouTube is very popular and many people like to download the videos from YouTube. Unfortunately, this is not as straightforward as it sounds, since there is no YouTube downloader built into Safari. A number of browsers, including Safari, have add-ons which allow YouTube videos to be downloaded. In addition, there are third-party apps where you can drop-in the YouTube URL and the app will go to YouTube and download the video for you. One such app is iFunia, which you can download from *ifunia.com*.

Installation is very straightforward and you simply drop the URL onto the interface and iFunia does the work for you.

4 Networking Tricks

Networking causes confusion, especially in the Windows world. Mac OS X makes networking very straightforward and in this chapter you will learn how to connect to your Mac from anywhere, connect easily to Wi-Fi networks, share wireless connections, and other networking tricks.

Access your Mac anywhere

This works for PCs too but is more straightforward on the Mac. If you have a Mac at home and one at work you can connect one to the other to view files, drag-and-drop files from one to the other and, if you want to, you can even see the desktop on the remote Mac and run programs on it.

Using Back to My Mac

This is the easiest method to use. You need to ensure Back to My Mac is enabled on both the local and the remote Macs.

 Go to **Apple Menu > System Preferences > iCloud**

2 Scroll down until you see **Back to My Mac** and make sure the check box is **checked**

Viewing folders and files on the remote Mac

If you only want to look at folders and files (rather than view the screen):

1 **Open a Finder window**

2 Look down the Sidebar and you should see the remote Mac listed under Shared

3 Click on your remote Mac and you will see various folders

4 Click the one you want to connect to

5 You can then browse folders and files

Copying folders or files to your local desktop

Simply drag from the remote window to your local Mac and the files will copy across to the local desktop. You can drag files the other way too, from the local Mac to the remote Mac.

The remote folder you are browsing will be shown on the desktop like this:

Viewing Remote Desktop

If you want to see the actual desktop of your remote Mac, rather than just the folders and files, it's very easy to do.

 Click on the remote Mac in the Sidebar

 When the window opens click **Share Screen...**

 The Screen-sharing app will open and you will see the login screen of the remote Mac

 Enter your usual **password** and the desktop will then be visible

The login screen of the remote Mac

Beware

Don't ever be tempted to do a restart on the remote Mac. You will never be able to screen share until you have logged in to your account and you cannot do that remotely! You have been warned!

Connect using an iPad or iPhone

You don't need another Mac or PC to connect to your Mac – you can use a VNC *(Virtual Network Computing)* app on your iOS or other handheld device to connect to a remote Mac or PC. There are various VNC apps available – search for "VNC" on the App Store. The example used here uses *Screens*.

Usually you need to know the IP address that your local Mac uses (*www.whatismyipaddress.com*). Once you know that, you can enter those details into your VNC app and connect to the Mac.

 Open the VNC app on the mobile device

2 Enter the **IP address** of the remote machine

3 At the login screen enter your **admin password** to control the remote Mac or PC

Login screen of the remote Mac

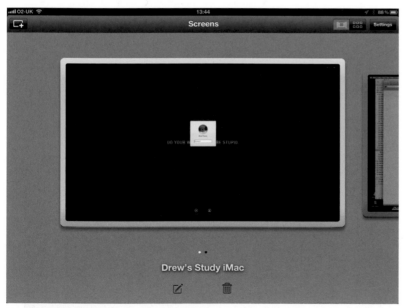

Waiting for password to be entered.

Once logged in you can use the remote Mac as if it were the local Mac.

Connect to Wi-Fi

Connecting to Wi-Fi using a Mac is very easy. Use the Wi-Fi tool on the menu bar and a dropdown menu will appear listing all those wireless networks available. If a network is open there will be no padlock, and if secure a padlock icon will be shown.

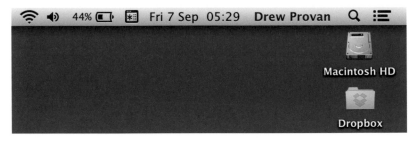

All available Wi-Fi networks near you will show up in the list.

> **1** Choose the one you want to connect to

If the Wi-Fi is secure you will be prompted for the password.

> **2** Enter the password set for your Wi-Fi network.

If Wi-Fi misbehaves

Sometimes things go wrong and the Wi-Fi does not behave normally. Simply switch Wi-Fi off and leave for 15 seconds then switch on and reconnect. That usually solves the problem.

Get Online using Mobile Phone

Some mobile phone tariffs include tethering or Personal Hotspot which means you can use your phone's 3G/4G connection for your laptop. The phone broadcasts its 3G/4G and the laptop joins this, after which you can browse the web, send and receive emails, etc. But beware, if you have a fixed data allowance in your contract you may use up your whole allowance. This is best only used in an emergency!

Set up Personal Hotspot

1 In the Settings app of the iPhone go to **Personal Hotspot** and activate this

```
Wi-Fi: On
Turn Wi-Fi Off

✓ NETGEAR-2.4-G              🔒 🛜
  BTHub3-FK66                🔒 🛜
  BTHub3-GJ39                🔒 🛜
  BTWiFi                        🛜
  BTWiFi-with-FON               🛜
  devolo-000B3BD42C7A        🔒 🛜
  Drew's iPhone              🔒 ⬯
  NETGEAR-DualBand-N         🔒 🛜
  SKYBC588                   🔒 🛜
  TALKTALK-FEC10D            🔒 🛜

Join Other Network...
Create Network...
Open Network Preferences...
```

2 You will be shown the password for the Hotspot. When you look for the phone's Hotspot in your Wi-Fi settings on the laptop, you will need to enter this password to get online

```
🛜   The Wi-Fi network "Drew's iPhone" requires a
     WPA2 password.

Password: [                    ]
          ☐ Show password
          ☑ Remember this network

(?)                    Cancel    Join
```

Beware

Using Personal Hotspot will eat into the data allowance on your phone. Use this option sparingly!

Share your Wi-Fi Connection

ISPs don't like this trick much, since it involves you picking up their network then broadcasting it for others to use. Why would you want to use this? Sometimes you have a connection in a hotel which is wired, and you have a laptop and a mobile device, or two of you have laptops but only one can be connected to Ethernet. Sharing your Wi-Fi connection enables one of you to be hard-wired to the network and broadcast a wireless signal so the other laptop can get online!

This is much easier to do on a Mac than a PC. On the PC side you will be setting up an *ad hoc* network.

On a Mac

1 **Click on the wi-fi icon** on the menu bar

2 Select **Create Network**

3 A window opens showing the network name (you can change the name)

4 Choose **40-bit WEP** protection (requires a five-character password)

5 Once set up, on the unconnected Mac go to Wi-Fi on the menu bar and **look for that network**. Enter the password and join the network

Beware

ISPs do not like you setting up ad hoc wireless networks. Use with caution!

Beware

Windows computers may have trouble logging in if you use 40-bit WEP, since this is an old security method. Windows prefers WPA.

98

Anonymous Surfing

Sometimes you want to surf the web without leaving the usual traces of your activities. There are apps you can buy that will hide your IP address and provide a false one (e.g. *Netshade*). But you can surf anonymously using most web browsers.

Safari

1   **Open Safari**

2   Click **Safari > Private Browsing...**

Now when you browse, no history will be left behind.

About Safari	
Safari Extensions...	
Preferences...	⌘,
Private Browsing...	
Reset Safari...	
Services	▶
Hide Safari	⌘H
Hide Others	⌥⌘H
Show All	
Quit Safari	⌘Q

Google Chrome

1   **Open Google Chrome**

2   Select **File > New Incognito Window**

New Tab	⌘T
New Window	⌘N
New Incognito Window	⇧⌘N
Reopen Closed Tab	⇧⌘T
Open File...	⌘O
Open Location...	⌘L
Close Window	⇧⌘W
Close Tab	⌘W
Save Page As...	⌘S
Email Page Location	⇧⌘I
Print...	⌘P

Network Utility

You will find this app in the Utilities folder. This lets you monitor network activity, "Finger" people, "Ping" websites, and many other fancy networking tricks.

 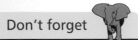

5 Printing Tricks

Like networking, Mac OS X makes printing a breeze. In this section we will look at printing tricks, setting up user-defined presets, and creating PDFs perfectly.

Printer Drivers

With modern computers, and Macs in particular, adding printer software to your computer is incredibly easy. Gone are the days when you had to install printer drivers from CDs supplied with your printer.

Installing a printer on the Mac

1 Go to **Apple Menu > System Preferences > Print & Scan**

Hot tip

If a printer misbehaves, delete it and reinstall it.

2 In the window that opens to add a printer click the + symbol and select **Add Printer or Scanner...**

3 You will then be shown a list of available printers. Even if your Mac does not have the drivers for these, clicking on one of these printers will force the Mac to connect to the Internet to download the required software

4 Once the window shows the name, location, etc., click **Add** and the printer driver will be installed for you

5 Close the window and start printing

Exploring Printing Options

When you print on the Mac a print dialog box will open. Most likely this will be the simplified dialog box. There will be times when you want to change the layout, page range, color and quality options, and many other variables. In order to do this you must click the **Show Details** button at the bottom of the print dialog box. Two thirds of the way down the window you will see the name of the application, in this case Safari, and below this is a drop-down menu where you can change many aspects of the printouts. You should explore these on an app-by-app basis.

Expand print panel by default

Use **Terminal** and type:

```
defaults write NSGlobalDomain
PMPrintingExpandedStateForPrint -bool true
```

Simplified print dialog box

...cont'd

Expanded print dialog box showing two pages per sheet

Expanded print dialog box showing booklet-printing options

Print to PDF

PDF (*Portable Document Format*) files are popular because they let someone view your document even if you created it using software the recipient does not have. With recent versions of OS X, an inbuilt PDF generator makes it incredibly easy to create a PDF file.

Sometimes your document may contain lots of images or photos which will make the PDF huge (and difficult to email). You will need to reduce the size of the PDF to make it more user-friendly (see Page 106).

Create a PDF file

1 Go to **Print** and select the **PDF** option

2 The file will be saved to the Desktop or other specified location

Viewing the PDF

In OS X, *Preview* is the default PDF viewer. You can change this to Acrobat Reader or another PDF viewer by right-clicking the PDF file and selecting another app.

Shrink the size of the PDF

1   Open the file in Preview and go to **File > Export...**

2   Choose the **Quartz Filter > Reduce File Size**

Hot tip

Reducing the size of your PDF will make it easier to email.

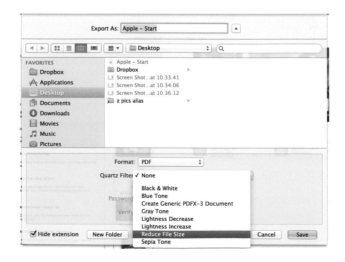

Create User Presets

If you regularly print in a certain way, e.g. landscape, two pages per sheet, or use other settings in the print dialog box each time you print, you can save these as a preset so that each time you print you can simply choose your preset then all the settings will be there.

For example, to proofread a book like this I use landscape, two pages per sheet with crop marks and other features. It is a chore setting this up each time so I saved these settings as a preset:

 Go to **Print > Detailed print dialog box**

 Enter all the settings you wish to use

 Click **Save Preset** and give it a **name**

 Each time you want to access those presets simply choose that preset

107

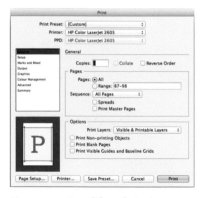

Default preset. This is what you would see if you choose Print. There are no special layout or other features specified.

User preset, with printer's crop marks, two pages per sheet in layout mode, high resolution etc. Once set up, these have been stored as my user preset and I can call it up each time I want to print sections of the book or even the entire book.

Save Paper and Ink!

Many printers allow draft printing (using less ink). The output does not look particularly great but if you simply want to proofread something, you don't need to have everything printed at high resolution. In addition, draft printing is faster than full resolution, especially if you have many images or photos in the document.

Apps to save printing costs

There are some free and paid apps that let you print many pages per sheet using less ink, for proofreading. *PagePacker* is one such app, which is easy to use but only prints eight pages at a time. To print more pages, use Preview and under the printer presets choose nine or 16 pages per sheet.

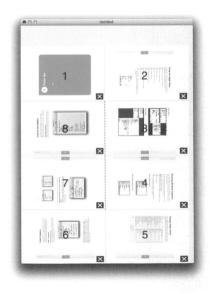

6 Font Management

With OS X, font management has become more tricky, with fonts scattered across the system in various locations. In this chapter we will look at optimizing font management and also how to switch off unwanted fonts.

Font Book

This app comes built in to OS X. It is a font viewer which lets you browse through your fonts and deactivate those you don't need. It also lets you view styles before you use them in a document.

Viewing your fonts

1 **Open Font Book**

2 **Scroll** through your list of fonts to view

3 **Click the black triangles** on the left to open the font family and see all available installed fonts

Viewing fonts different ways

You can view as a simple alphabet (as shown above), or you can show all available characters in a particular typeface as shown on the next page.

Hot tip

Try to deactivate any fonts you are not likely to use.

Beware

Some fonts (though they may look very foreign to you) are actually needed by the system. If a warning box comes up telling you that, do not deactivate that font.

Custom view

1 Open Font Book and go to **Preview Custom** (⌘ + 3)

2 Scroll to the bottom of the text in the viewer and **type or paste in your own text** which will be displayed in the selected font

Where to store Fonts

Prior to OS X you had to store Mac fonts in one folder, the Fonts folder. With OS X you can pretty much store your fonts anywhere. The Mac will find them and use them wherever they are. Lots of apps install their own fonts, e.g. Microsoft Office, Adobe Creative Suite, and many others. Sometimes the fonts are stored in the main Font Library, and sometimes in the app's own Font folder.

The three main locations are:

- Main Library
- User Library
- App Folder

Having fonts in multiple locations can cause duplicate entries. This may cause you to encounter various problems (e.g. crashes) that will need to be resolved.

This is where the Main Library keeps its fonts

User fonts are kept here

And an app such as Adobe Creative Suite keeps its own fonts here

Disable (Deactivate) Fonts!

The Mac already comes with a fair number of fonts. As you install more apps, you will install their associated fonts. This will result in your Mac having to keep track of potentially hundreds of different fonts. Although it is great to have lots of fonts, you are not likely to use the vast majority of these. For this reason, it is best to deactivate any that you are not likely to need. This should speed up your Mac a little since it is having to keep track of fewer typefaces.

To disable a font

 Open Font Book and review your list of fonts in the left pane (All Fonts)

 Look at the typeface by selecting the font and looking at the Preview on the right

 To disable the font go to **Edit > Disable**

 You will be asked *Are you sure you want to disable the selected fonts?* Click **Disable**

The font will now be marked *Off.*

Resolve Duplicate Fonts

As mentioned earlier, you will at some point end up with duplicate fonts. When you open Font Book you may see a yellow warning triangle alerting you to the fact that a font has duplicate entries.

It is always best to resolve this by disabling and removing (to the Trash) the duplicate font.

To remove duplicate font

1 **Open Font Book**

2 View the list of fonts and check to see if you have any yellow warning triangles

3 **Click the black triangle** to view the fonts and see which ones are duplicated

4 Click **Resolve Automatically** (which is the easiest method) unless you want to do them by one-by-one

Hot tip

Remove duplicates to keep your Mac running smoothly and prevent crashes.

Accessing Special Characters

You may be working on a technical document and require special characters, such as arrows, symbols, Greek letters, or other characters not shown on the main keyboard.

Accessing special characters

1 Go to **System Preferences** and click **Keyboard**

2 Make sure **Show Keyboards & Character Viewers in menu bar** is checked. You should then see the Character Viewer at the top right of the menu bar

3 Click the keyboard icon on the menu bar and choose **Show Character Viewer**

4 A window will open showing various special characters, including arrows, parentheses, Currency Symbols Pictographs, etc.

5 Look for the type of symbol you wish to use and find the one you want. With your cursor in your document at the correct place that you wish to have the special character, double-click the symbol in the character viewer window. The character will now be pasted into your text

7 Personalizing your Mac

Like home decorating, you will want to have your Mac looking exactly the way you want. In this section we will explore the various options for wallpapers and screensavers, clock display, sounds, icon size, and more.

Customize the Login Screen

You can change many aspects of the Mac's look and feel, starting with the login screen (the one you see when you start the Mac).

Add a message to the Login window

This Terminal command enables you to add a message of your choice to the login window.

```
sudo defaults write /Library/Preferences/com.
apple.loginwindow LoginwindowText "Your Message"
```

Replace "Your Message" with the message of your choice. Don't make it too long. To revert back to the default:

```
sudo defaults write /Library/Preferences/com.
apple.loginwindow LoginwindowText ""
```

Disable Automatic login?

Logging in automatically saves you time but means your Mac is accessible to anyone. It is better to disable Automatic Login, which means you must enter your administrator password to access the Mac.

To switch Automatic Login on and off

1 Go to **System Preferences > Users & Groups**

2 Click your account name and select **Login Options**

Beware

Sudo commands can be dangerous so use with care.

Beware

Automatic login saves time but allows anyone to log in and see all your files!

118

Change the Clock

The menu bar clock can be configured in a variety of ways

- Digital or analog
- Display the time with seconds
- Several other options

To change the configuration

1 Go to **System Preferences > Date & Time**

2 Click the **Clock** tab on the right

3 Check or uncheck until the clock is the way you want it

Analog clock

Wallpapers

Wallpaper is basically the term given to the picture which appears on your Mac's desktop. The wallpaper images are stored within your pictures folder.

You can also access the images supplied by Apple which are shown in the window on the left (**System Preferences > Desktop & Screen Saver**).

To change the desktop image

1 Open **Desktop & Screen Saver**

2 Make sure the **Desktop** button is active

3 Select the image you wish to use from the folders on the left under Apple (*Nature, Plants, etc.*)

4 You can also choose images from your iPhoto folder or from any other third party source, e.g. *interfacelift.com*

Screen Savers

In the old days, if you left an image on the screen for too long it would leave a permanent image on your screen. In order to avoid this, screen savers were developed to create a moving image which would prevent screen burnout.

Apple provides a number of screen saver options

1 Go to **System Preferences > Desktop & Screen Saver**

2 Click on **Screen Saver**

3 Choose from the various options depending on your personal taste

4 You can even generate your own message to be displayed when your Mac goes to sleep (Click Screen Saver Options)

Security
If you are away from your Mac and the screen saver kicks in, it is a good idea to force the Mac to use a password to wake it up. Otherwise, anyone can view your files when you are away from your Mac.

Desktop Icon Size

The desktop icons can be made larger or smaller and can even be configured to take up a specific layout.

Adjusting the size and layout of the desktop icons

1 Go to **View > Options**

2 Adjust size of the icons by using the **slider bar** – moving it **left or right**

3 Adjust **Grid spacing**

4 You can alter other settings, e.g. the size and position of the text, and whether to show icon preview

Desktop

Icon size: 36 × 36

Grid spacing:

Text size: 12

Label position:
● Bottom ○ Right

☐ Show item info
☑ Show icon preview
Sort by: None

Notifications

Notifications are very useful if you want to be reminded about calendar events, new tweets, and other incoming data. However, with several apps having access to Notifications, you could be inundated with notifications all day long.

For this reason, it is useful to prune notifications using:

1 System **Preferences > Notifications**

2 Scroll down through the list of apps using the Notification Center in the left-hand pane in the window

3 Click on each one individually and see how notifications are shown

4 If you want to disable notifications, simply click **None** and that app will not send a notification

5 If you prefer banners in the middle of the screen, select **Banners** and if you prefer alerts to be shown at the top right of the screen, click **Alerts**

Save Energy using Energy Saver

Saving energy is important, especially when using a laptop. By adjusting the Energy Saver System Preferences you can control when your Mac goes to sleep, when the hard drive spins down, and other energy-saving features.

1 Go to **System Preferences > Energy Saver**

2 Review the options shown in the window

3 Putting the computer to **sleep** for around 10–15 minutes is fine, and you can adjust the display sleep time to suit your needs – usually two or three minutes would be long enough

4 You can ask the Mac to put the **hard disks** to sleep wherever possible to save power, and you can also allow the Mac to dim the screen slightly whilst running on battery power to save some energy

5 If you enable **Power Nap** while running on battery power this will let your Mac check for new emails and other events even while asleep

It is a good idea to show your **Battery Status** in the menu bar. Checking this box will show all the battery power remaining as an icon and also as a percentage.

System Sounds

The Mac has a number of sounds built into the system which are associated with various alerts on the Mac.

Changing the alert sound

1 Go to **System Preferences > Sound**

2 Scroll through the various alert sounds provided and choose the one you want

3 You can also adjust the **Alert volume** and **Output volume**

4 You can also **mute** the Mac from here

This System Preference also controls the Output, letting you choose between the built-in internal speakers or, if you have Apple TV, you can use AirPlay to listen to music and other sounds on a TV.

You can also plug in microphones and other peripherals such as keyboards and select those as the sound input device.

Bring Back Save As...

With OS X 10.7 (Lion) Apple changed the way files are saved, removing Save As... from the File menu. Many people have expressed a desire to bring this back and with 10.8 you can reactivate Save As... (allows you to open a document, edit it and save as a different name).

To use Save As...

The old way of doing this was **Shift + Command + S**, (or it could be accessed directly from the File menu). With Mountain Lion you need to press **Shift + Command + S** and then press **Option**. Duplicate will change to Save As...

This is slightly cumbersome and you can change to a full restore of Save As...

The only problem with this is that the edits you make to the second document are transferred to the *original* document. So this is still *not* a true Save As... *(correct at the time of printing)*.

Create a new shortcut for Duplicate

Open the Keyboard system preferences and go to the Keyboard Shortcuts tab. Select the Application Shortcuts section and then click the **+** button to create a new shortcut for all applications. In the menu title field type *Duplicate* and then set a shortcut of your choosing for this feature, e.g. Shift + Command + D or Option + Shift + Command + S.

8 Mac Maintenance

The Mac does not require much maintenance but over time you will accumulate large cache files. In this section you will learn about general maintenance, clearing temporary and other unwanted stuff from your Mac, backing up, defragmenting your hard drive, and installing and uninstalling software cleanly.

General Maintenance

Macs do not need much looking after, although in the past we were advised to defragment our hard drives and carry out other household cleaning tasks. Now with OS X there is little that needs doing on a regular basis.

After installing lots of apps, using apps and browsing the web, your Mac will accumulate various temporary files and folders, as well as caches of websites and other log files. There is a view that, over time, these can slow your Mac down, hence various apps have been developed to remove this unwanted clutter easily.

Maintenance worth carrying out

- Clearing Safari history and caches

- Clearing cookies from Safari and other browsers

- Clearing old logs and User cache folder

Manually clearing out the User Cache file
This is found in your User library:

1   **Go > Library** (you may need to hold down the **Option** key when you click Go since the User Library is hidden by default)

2   Select the entire contents of the folder and drag to Trash or right-click and select **Move to Trash**

3   **Empty Trash**

Automate the Cleaning!

There are several apps that can clear out all of the unwanted files. Some are free and others are paid apps.

Three useful maintenance apps

- CCleaner (*http://www.piriform.com/CCLEANER*, free)

- OnyX (*http://www.onyxmac.com*, free)

- MainMenu (*http://mainmenuapp.com*, paid)

CCleaner

CCleaner is a very simple app, ported over from Windows. It carries out a very limited range of cleaning functions and does not clean out the User cache. It does, however, deal with Internet debris and temporary browser files pretty well.

CCleaner's main window

Other tools including Uninstaller

OnyX & MainMenu

These are more powerful than CCleaner but perform similar functions.

MainMenu

Batch tasks are configured using this window:

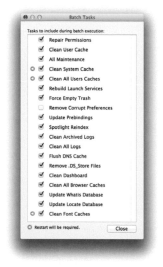

OnyX cleaning options

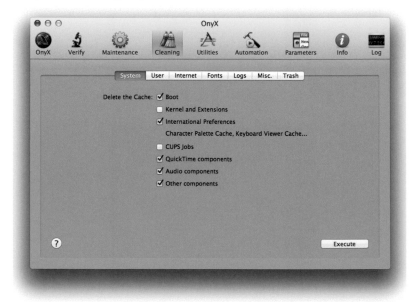

Time Machine

All drives fail eventually so you should plan for this. If you have no backups then you may lose everything – photos, music, documents and much more. Everyone who uses a computer should back up regularly!

OS X includes a great app, Time Machine, which copies your files to an external disk every hour so if something goes wrong, e.g. a file gets lost or becomes corrupt, you can go back in time, find the file and bring it back!

To make best use of Time Machine you should have a 1–2 GB drive at least, plugged into your main Mac. If you have an iMac and a MacBook Pro you can back up using the wired route for the iMac and wireless for the MacBook Pro.

Setting up Time Machine

 1 Attach an **external drive** to your Mac

2 Open **Time Machine**

3 **Choose the disk** you want to use for backing up

...cont'd

 Time Machine will prepare the drive (ie. format it) and will then do a complete backup of your Mac

5 It will then do hourly incremental backups as long as the Mac is running

To restore a corrupted or lost file

1 **Run Time Machine**

2 The Time Machine window will open and you will see the dates running along the right edge of the screen

3 **Locate the folder** where the file is, click an earlier date and Time Machine will go back in time to find the earlier version of the file

4 Once you find it, click it once and click **Restore**

5 The file will be restored to the Desktop

Backup Everything?

There is no need to backup all your files. You don't need Time Machine to regularly backup applications and Library files because this will make the backups slow. Library files can be huge and changing one item, even if very small, will force the whole file to be backed up.

Choose which items not to backup

1 Open Time Capsule **Preferences**

2 Click **Options**

3 You will see a window called **Exclude these items from backups:**

4 **Click the + symbol** and add your User Library folder, Applications and any other things you don't want to backup (e.g. external USB drives)

5 You will save time and lots of disk space if you backup the items that really need backing up, e.g. documents

Hot tip

Selected backups are more sensible than total "kitchen sink" backups!

Time Machine

Show All

Exclude these items from backups:

TimeMachine backups	986.1 GB
/Applications	Calculating...
System Files and Applications	124.7 MB

+ −   Calculating size of full backup...

☑ Notify after old backups are deleted

Time M

OFF

? Cancel Save   omes full.

Click the lock to prevent further changes.

☑ Show Time Machine in menu bar   Options... ?

Other Backup Solutions

Simple copy

A cheap (*but risky*) strategy for backing up can be achieved by simply dragging your Home folder or Documents folder to a USB or removable drive.

The downside of this method is that you need to remember to do it. If you have large iPhoto libraries, or iTunes collections you will need a large drive to copy to. The process will take some time because there will be many gigabytes of data to copy across. But at least doing this occasionally means you don't lose everything if your hard drive fails.

To backup the folder (on the left) to the USB drive (on the right)...

Drag-and-drop the folder onto the USB drive and the folder will be copied

Recovering files

If you accidentally delete a file and you haven't emptied the Trash, it is easy to retrieve the file. If you have emptied the Trash the situation becomes more complex!

Options for salvaging lost files

1. Time Machine – if you were wise and set up Time Machine, you can go back in time and grab a copy of your file

2. Paid recovery apps, e.g. DataRescue, Disk Drill, Super Duper, and others

Backup Apps

There are several on the market. The advantage of these is that you can usually set up a schedule for your backup, and tell the app which files and folders you want to backup. You can do a timed backup (e.g. every day at a set time), or each time you plug the USB drive into your Mac the backup software will detect this and perform a backup for you. Any files you have added or changed will be updated so you will always have a copy of your most current documents.

Examples of paid apps include: ChronoSync, Data Backup, Tri-BACKUP, SuperDuper!, Synk Standard, Knox, SmartBackup, and Synchronize! X Plus.

ChronoSync

You can download a trial from *http://www.econtechnologies.com/pages/support/demo_form.php*.

In the ChronoSync window (above) you can see the Left Target (the data you want to copy) being copied in one direction to the drive on the right (Right Target).

Defragmenting your Drive

Hard drives can become fragmented over time. This is because as the drives fill up, there is no space to write large files so they end up being split into several parts across the drive. When you open the file, the Mac has to look around for all the pieces and join these in order to open the file.

Historically, both on PCs and Macs people have defragmented their drives periodically, using apps that move files around and join up split files. But there are two schools of thought with Macs: you do not need to defragment drives running OS X, and others who think you do. Randy B. Singer, author of *The Macintosh Bible*, has written about this on his website (*http://www.macattorney. com*) and is a firm believer that defragmentation is useful.

Note: there is no defragmentation app built into OS X (unlike Windows which includes an app to defragment your drive).

iDefrag

There are several apps available for defragmenting drives running OS X. iDefrag (*http://www.coriolis-systems.com/iDefrag.php*) is probably the best.

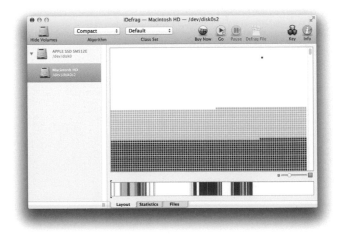

iDefrag window showing the status of the drive before defragmenting.

Clear the Desktop!

The Mac has to keep track of many items and the Desktop is one of them. The more files and folders you have on the Desktop, the harder the Mac has to work to keep track of all these files. With the speed-increases seen with newer Macs you may not notice the slowdown so much, but it is good practice to keep your Desktop as clear as you can.

You should keep *only* those items you need regular access to on the Desktop. In fact, many of these can be added to the Sidebar rather than dropped onto the Desktop. By default, a new Mac will have nothing showing on the Desktop, not even the hard disk icon!

How to keep the Desktop clear

1. Regularly file your documents in the Documents folder (create subfolders within the Documents folder)

2. If you must keep some items on the Desktop, consider creating a folder on the Desktop and dropping them into that

3. Try creating aliases for frequently-accessed folders

Install an Antivirus App?

Do you need an antivirus app for the Mac? Yes and no. There are few viruses around for Macs, though this may change with the increasing popularity of Macs. So, although your Mac is unlikely to be infected by a virus, someone could send you one in an email and you could pass it to others.

An antivirus app would detect the virus before you passed it to someone else.

What antivirus apps are available for the Mac?

1. Norton AntiVirus

2. McAfee VirusScan for Mac

3. ProtectMac

4. iAntiVirus

5. VirusBarrier X6

6. ClamXav 2 (*http://www.clamxav.com*). This is an unobtrusive *free* antivirus app and the one I would suggest you install

Hot tip

ClamXav is a perfectly good (and free) anti-virus app for the Mac.

ClamXav found two phishing emails on my Mac!

Repair Disk Permissions

OS X is based on UNIX and it is advised that we should rebuild disk permissions on a regular (maybe weekly) basis. The reasons for doing this are complex but, luckily, the process of repairing permissions is very straightforward.

Many apps (OnyX, MainMenu, and others) will help you repair permissions but the easiest way is to use Disk Utility which comes with OS X.

Repairing Disk Permissions

1 Go to **Utilities > Disk Utility**

2 Open Disk Utility, choose the drive in the pane on the left and click **Verify Disk Permissions**

3 If errors are reported, click **Repair Disk Permissions**

Rebuild Spotlight Database

Spotlight keeps tons of information about your Mac stored in a database which contains titles of files and folders along with their location, plus all the searchable text within files. Every now and again it is a good idea to rebuild this to keep it fully up to date.

Checkout Spotlight's preferences so you can see the order in which search results are displayed (you can alter the order). You can also stop Spotlight searching specific drives, files or folders (see the **Privacy** tab).

Rebuild the Spotlight database

1 Many apps will do it for you (MainMenu, OnyX, etc.)

2 **Open Spotlight**

3 Click **Privacy** and *drag your hard drive onto it* (sounds drastic but it's fine!)

4 Quit and relaunch **System Preferences > Spotlight**

5 Click **Privacy** and deselect your hard drive (click the **minus** symbol)

6 The database will be entirely rebuilt

Rebuild Mail Database

Apple Mail will sometimes slow down if you store large numbers of emails and have lots of subfolders within the app. Similar to Spotlight, it is a good idea to rebuild Mail's database so it can recatalog all your emails.

Rebuilding the Mail database

 Open Mail and go to **Mailbox > Erase Deleted Items > In All Accounts...**

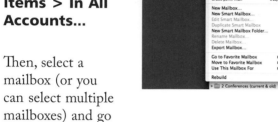

Then, select a mailbox (or you can select multiple mailboxes) and go to **Mailbox > Rebuild**

Mail will run faster if you rebuild its database regularly.

Installers

Many programs will include installers; apps that place the app in the Applications Folder and install associated files in the required locations. Installers are recognized by a distinctive file such as .pkg (package). Once you double-click the .pkg file a script will take you through the entire install procedure, making the whole process as easy as possible.

Click the **.dmg file** and the disk image opens to reveal:

after which the installer script leads you step-by-step through the installation.

Uninstalling Apps

This is arguably easier on the PC than the Mac, since OS X does not have an uninstaller Control Panel. Uninstalling cleanly is important because solely removing the app will generally leave other associated files hanging around. It is best to remove the app *and* all of its associated files.

There are three main ways to uninstall apps

- **Drag the app** to the Trash

- Use the **dedicated uninstaller** app that came with the app (most apps do not have uninstallers)

- **Use an app** onto which you can drag the unwanted app and the uninstaller app will search the drive for associated files and put all of these in the Trash

Dragging the app to the Trash

This is probably fine for most apps. Although associated files are left behind, the chances are these won't cause any problems so you can just leave them there. But if you install a lot of apps this could potentially leave many orphaned files lying around when you trash the apps. This is the simplest method of removing apps and one that Apple would probably recommend.

Using dedicated uninstaller apps

Some programs come with uninstallers designed to round-up the app and its associated files and trash the lot if you decide to remove the app from your Mac.

Beware

Most apps on the Mac do not come with uninstallers (unlike Windows where uninstallers are common).

143

Name Adobe AIR Uninstaller
Kind Application
Size 62.3 MB
Created Thursday, 28 June 2012 07:18
Modified Thursday, 28 June 2012 07:18
Last opened Thursday, 28 June 2012 07:18
Version 3.3

Adobe LIghtroom has a dedicated uninstaller. Double-click this file and a dialog window opens (right)

The dialog window leads you through the uninstall process

Uninstaller Apps

A number of third party shareware or freeware apps can help you find an app's files and trash them. These apps may not remove 100% of the associated files but they do a pretty good job:

- AppCleaner
- AppZapper
- AppTrap
- CleanApp
- TrashMe

AppCleaner

Opening AppCleaner, then dropping an app onto the window allows you to see the app with all of its associated files before you click Delete and send the whole lot to the Trash.

9 Running Windows or Linux

Many people need to run Windows applications and the Mac is a great computer for running Windows. This section shows you various options for installing Windows on a Mac. You can run other operating systems as well, such as Linux, and we will have a look at how you get Linux up and running on the Mac.

Running Windows on the Mac

Because Macs use Intel chips you can run Windows on the Mac using a variety of methods:

- Boot Camp

- Virtualization

- Other methods, e.g. CrossOver

Boot Camp allows you to boot the Mac directly into Windows, which effectively makes the Mac a PC. If you want true Windows functionality and speed this is arguably the best option to use.

If you choose virtualization (*Parallels* or *VMWare Fusion*), you create a Windows partition on your Mac hard drive and run Windows from there, making Windows a virtual computer. You can run Mac and Windows apps side by side.

There are alternative solutions on offer (e.g. *CrossOver*, *http://www.codeweavers.com/products/* or *https://www.virtualbox.org*) which let you run Windows apps on the Mac, but the Mac will not behave quite like a PC and this is probably the least satisfactory solution.

Using Boot Camp means you must boot into either Windows or Mac at startup – but you can't have both at the same time.

For the first two options, you will need to buy a copy of Windows to install on the Mac, since these are not supplied by Apple or third parties.

RAM
If you want to run Windows smoothly on the Mac, especially with the virtualization option, make sure you have plenty of RAM! The more you have, the better the experience will be.

Boot Camp

This is the method that lets you run Windows pretty much as if you are using a PC rather than a Mac.
The Boot Camp installer is located in your Utilities folder.

Installing Boot Camp

Boot Camp Assistant

1 Go to **Utilities > Boot Camp Assistant**

2 Run the app and follow the instructions

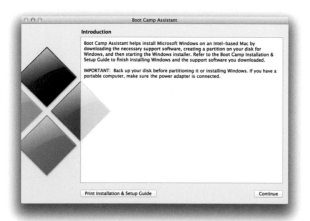

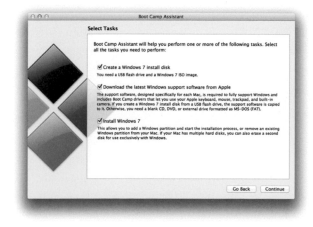

...cont'd

Decide whether you want a bootable version of Windows on USB

You may not need this, but if you want a version of Windows that can boot from USB, select this option and follow the instructions.

Make sure there is a USB drive attached to your Mac and Boot Camp Assistant will format the USB drive.

Boot Camp Assistant will let you set up the Windows partition to the size you choose. Decide on the partition size you want, then use the slider to set this up.

You will then be asked to insert your Windows installer disk and will be taken through the setup as you would on any PC.

Boot into Windows at startup

You must tell the Mac which OS you want to start up in. When you start the Mac hold down the **Option** key and you will see the Mac and the Windows drives. Use the arrow keys then hit Enter to boot up into either Mac or PC.

Once booted into Windows, your Mac will look like a regular PC.

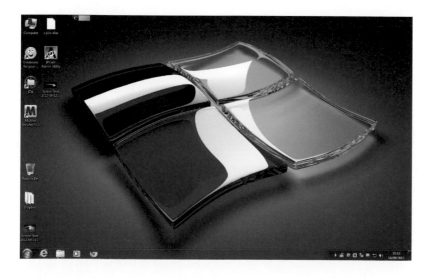

Virtualization

This is a complicated subject, but in essence, virtualization software lets you run Windows or another operating system alongside Mac OS X. You can run in full screen mode so your Mac will look like a PC but the speed may not be quite as good as it would be under Boot Camp.

PC gaming

If you want to play PC games, virtualization is not such a good option (install Boot Camp if gaming is your thing).

Importing an existing Boot Camp partition

If you already have a Boot Camp version of Windows you may be able to import this into VMWare Fusion or Parallels if you decide you no longer want to be forced into booting into either Windows or Mac at startup.

Two main contenders

- Parallels

- VMWare Fusion

VMWare Fusion

Beware

Virtual PCs are great but don't expect native PC speed (you need to use Boot Camp for this).

Parallels Virtualization

You can view a virtual PC in several ways

1. Windows Desktop running alongside Mac

2. Full screen (you cannot see Mac Desktop)

3. Coherence (Windows Desktop disappears but you can launch PC apps and run them ON the Mac desktop)

Below, you can see the Windows 7 desktop running on top of the Mac desktop (Parallels).

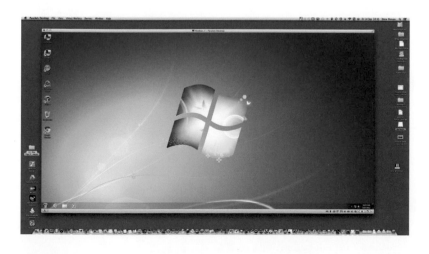

...cont'd

If you prefer not to see the Mac desktop you can enter full screen where Windows takes over the entire screen. Through sharing you can still access your Mac files and folders.

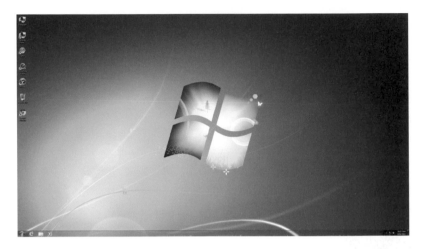

If you want to see only the Mac desktop but you still want to run Windows apps, you can use Coherence, which hides the PC side of things but still gives you full access to the Windows Start menu, and all of its apps.

In the figure below I am running Microsoft Publisher (a Windows-only app) right on my Mac Desktop as if it were a Mac app.

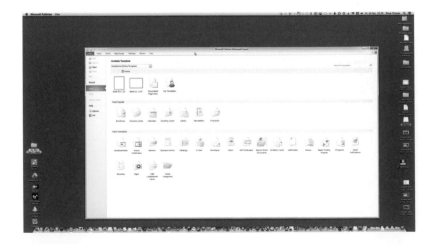

VMWare Fusion Views

You can run the same views in VMWare Fusion: single window (where you see Mac and Windows Desktops together), full screen or Unity (where the Windows Desktop is hidden but you can still run Windows apps).

Single window

The PC window runs on top of the Mac OS X window.

Full screen

In this view, the Mac desktop is hidden and Windows takes over the screen completely.

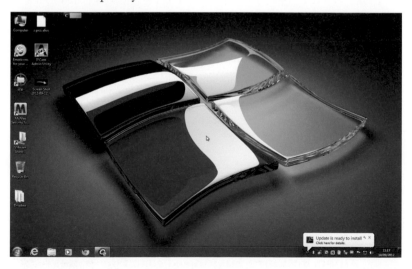

Installing Linux

Linux is another operating system which can run on the Mac. Although it uses a desktop and icons it is less intuitive than OS X or Windows. But the OS is "open source" which means that unlike OS X or Windows you can obtain this free of charge, in various versions. Much of the software that runs on Linux is also open source. If you are on a budget and want to save lots of money you might consider installing Linux.

Installing Linux (Ubuntu version)

1 **Format a USB drive** (Mac OS X journaled format)

2 **Download Ubuntu desktop** (*www.ubuntu.com/download*). Choose either 32- or 64-bit

3 Once downloaded, **copy the ISO file** from your Download folder to the USB drive. Alternatively, you could copy the ISO file to a CD

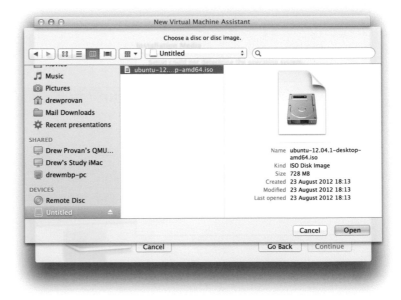

4 **Open VMWare Fusion** and go to **File > New**

5 Follow the on-screen instructions

6 Click **Continue without disc** to use a disc image

7 Click **Choose a disc or disc image**

...cont'd

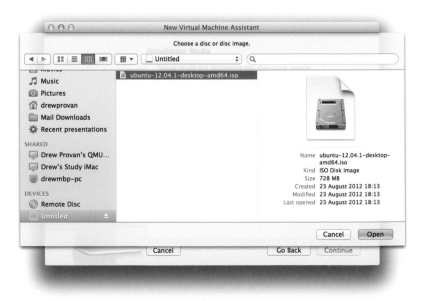

8 Navigate to the disc image on the USB drive **ubuntu–12.04.1–desktop–amd64.iso** then click **Open** then **Continue**

9 VMWare will recognise the OS as LINUX 64-bit if you chose this option

10 Click **Continue Easy Install**

11 Enter a **password** and confirm this

12 Make sure the Virtual Machine can **Read and Write**. Click **Continue**

13 VMWare will download the tools necessary to support Linux. Click **Download**

Running Ubuntu

 When you see the Finish window click **Finish**

 Change the name of the Virtual Machine if you wish to

Ubuntu will now boot up in a new window and install all the necessary software

As with VMWare (or Parallels) running Windows, you can run Ubuntu in single window mode (on top of Mac desktop), full screen, or Unity.

Here is the newly-installed Ubuntu in full screen mode

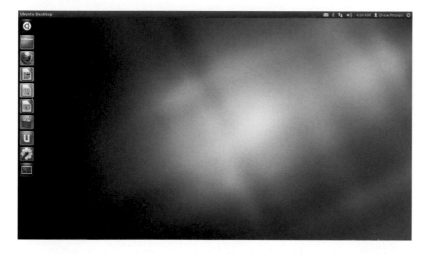

Single window mode (showing Ubuntu settings)

...cont'd

A number of apps are preinstalled with Ubuntu. The image below shows the free word processor, which is powerful and compatible with Microsoft Word.

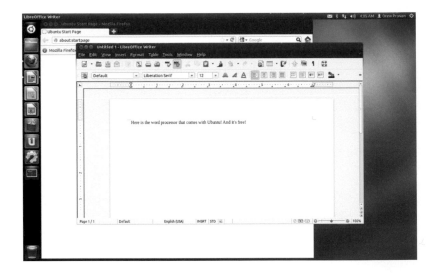

The Ubuntu Software Center is like the app store, with many apps that you can install.

10 Command Line Hacks

Using Linux commands may seem slightly arcane but there are many modifications you can make to OS X using the Command Line. In this section we will look at some Finder- and app-specific hacks you can make to your Mac.

Using Terminal commands

There are lots of apps that let you tinker under the hood with OS X, switching off and on various features. You can modify many aspects of the Mac using a Utility called *Terminal* (found in your Utilities folder). It allows you to type UNIX commands to the Mac. Unfortunately *Terminal* is not a very user-friendly app and you have to be sure of what you are doing if you enter such commands. A wrong command can render your Mac useless, so try these out with caution!

Some of the commands are very useful, e.g. converting Apple Mail-copied email addresses into a more useful form, and others control the behavior of the Finder or other graphical features.

For many of these hacks, if you wish to return your Mac to normal, replace **true** in the command with **false**, **YES** with **NO**, and **1** with **0**.

Many of the commands in the book wrap across two or more lines but when entering them in Terminal keep them on one line.

For many of these, you will need to log out and back in to your account to enable the changes.

Resources

There are many websites offering UNIX hacks for you to play with.

Finder Hacks

2D Dock
This changes the 3D dock to a flat 2D version. Copy and paste the following code into Terminal.

```
defaults write com.apple.dock no-glass -boolean
YES
```

```
killall Dock
```

Add a gradient behind a stack item
This enables you to put a small gradient behind an icon.

```
defaults write com.apple.dock mouse-over-hilte-
stack -boolean YES
```

```
killall Dock
```

Add a message to the Login window
This Terminal command enables you to add a message of your choice to the Login window. Sudo commands can be dangerous so *use with care!*

```
sudo defaults write /Library/Preferences/com.
apple.loginwindow LoginwindowText "Your Message"
```

Replace "Your Message" with the message of your choice – don't make it too long. To revert back to the default type the following code:

```
sudo defaults write /Library/Preferences/com.
apple.loginwindow LoginwindowText ""
```

...cont'd

Increase Dock magnification size

This hack lets you increase the size of the magnification of the Dock icons. Do not go higher than 512.

```
defaults write com.apple.dock largesize -int 512
```

Increase Desktop icon size

If you want massive icons on you Desktop this hack lets you increase the icons to 512 pixels x 512 pixels. This may slow down older machines.

```
defaults write com.apple.finder DesktopViewOptions
-dict IconSize -integer 512
```

```
killall Finder
```

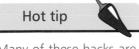

Hot tip

Many of these hacks are available using apps, e.g. TinkerTool and several others.

Changing the format of Screen Shots

You can change the default screenshot format to JPEG, TIFF, PNG, BMP, or GIF. You need to log out and back in again, or restart for the changes to take effect.

```
defaults write com.apple.screencapture type jpg
```

Change the Login picture

If you get bored with the Login screen, you can change it with this bit of code. Change the file location in the second half of the string to the exact file location of your chosen picture.

```
defaults write /Library/Preferences/com.apple.
loginwindow DesktopPicture "/System/Library/
CoreServices/Finder.app/Contents/Resources/
vortex.png"
```

Clear the Open With menu

If you right-click on a file you can open it with many applications. Sometimes your OS can get a little confused and list many applications. This hack clears this list and lets you start again.

```
/System/Library/Frameworks/CoreServices.
framework/Versions/A/Frameworks/
```

```
LaunchServices.framework/Versions/A/Support/
lsregister
```

```
-kill -r -domain local -domain system -domain
user
```

Window drag speed

This hack changes the time delay it takes to drag windows around in spaces; it's currently set to 0.75.

```
defaults write com.apple.dock workspaces-edge-
delay -float 0.5
```

Disable Dashboard

If you don't want or like the dashboard running, you can disable it. Change YES to NO to enable it again.

```
defaults write com.apple.dashboard mcx-disabled
-boolean YES
```

```
killall Dock
```

Enable Double Scroll Arrows

This hack enables the double arrow set for up and down, left or right, to be at both ends of the scroll bar. Use System Preferences to reset.

```
defaults write "Apple Global Domain"
AppleScrollBarVariant DoubleBoth
```

Increase the Dock size

This command enables you to change the size of the Dock. Use the sliders in System Preferences to reduce this size. Don't go larger than 256.

```
defaults write com.apple.dock tilesize -int 256
```

Disable the Crash Dialog box

This disables the Quit Dialog box when an application crashes. Type "prompt" to enable it again.

```
defaults write com.apple.CrashReporter DialogType
none
```

Drag a Widget onto the Desktop

This is a great hack, since it enables widgets to be placed onto the Desktop. Drag a widget around and press F12 to drag it onto the

Desktop. Repeat the process again to drag a widget back onto the dashboard. You may need to log off or restart for it to take effect.

```
defaults write com.apple.dashboard devmode YES
```

List all open files

```
lsof
```

Eject a CD...

CDs and DVDs can get stuck. This hack helps you eject the disk. *Note*: it may not always be Disk 1.

```
diskutil eject disk1
```

Count number of lines in the text in the Clipboard

```
pbpaste | wc -l
```

Count number of words in the text in the Clipboard

```
pbpaste | wc -w
```

Sort lines of text in the Clipboard and copy back to the Clipboard

```
pbpaste | sort | pbcopy
```

Reverse each line of text in the Clipboard

Makes each line appear backwards, and copies them back to the Clipboard.

```
pbpaste | rev | pbcopy
```

Strip duplicate lines from text in the Clipboard

```
pbpaste | sort | uniq | pbcopy
```

```
pbpaste | sort | uniq -d | pbcopy
```

```
pbpaste | sort | uniq -u | pbcopy
```

Tidy up HTML in the Clipboard and copy it back to the Clipboard

```
pbpaste | tidy | pbcopy
```

Display the first five lines from the Clipboard

```
pbpaste | head -n 5
```

Display the last five lines from the Clipboard

```
pbpaste | tail -n 5
```

Convert tabs to spaces for the lines in the Clipboard

```
pbpaste | expand | pbcopy
```

Display a history of commands used in the terminal by the current user

```
history
```

Convert a file to HTML

```
textutil -convert html file.extension
```

Nano (text editor)
For quick changes to text files.

```
nano [file_to_edit]
```

Use Control + O to Save and Control + X to quit.

```
clear
```

Key repeat rate
You can re-enable the repeat key presses (off by default) with this Terminal command.

```
defaults write -g ApplePressAndHoldEnabled -bool
false
```

To reverse replace the "false" at the end with a "true".

Disable Mountain Lion's window animations

```
defaults write NSGlobalDomain
NSAutomaticWindowAnimationsEnabled -bool false
```

To reverse replace "false" in the above command with "true".

Enable AirDrop on unsupported Macs and over Ethernet

AirDrop will only work with newer Macs and over Wi-Fi. If you wish to enable this feature on some older systems and over Ethernet, use this hack.

```
defaults write com.apple.NetworkBrowser
BrowseAllInterfaces -bool true
```

To return your Mac to normal, replace "true" in the above command with "false".

Disable Smooth Scrolling

Use this hack to switch off smooth scrolling. To return OS X to its pre-Smooth Scrolling functionality.

```
defaults write -g NSScrollAnimationEnabled -bool
NO
```

To enable Smooth Scrolling again, replace the "NO" in the above statement with "YES".

Disable Rubber Band Effect

```
defaults write -g NSScrollViewRubberbanding -int 0
```

This does not work for every app. You will need to restart apps on an app-by-app basis to see the change. Replace "0" in the above command with a "1" to re-enable the rubber band effect.

Check which Processes are using the Internet

```
lsof -P -i -n | cut -f 1 -d " " | uniq
```

Menu bar: disable Transparency

```
defaults write NSGlobalDomain
AppleEnableMenuBarTransparency -bool false
```

Menu bar: show remaining Battery Time; hide percentage

```
defaults write com.apple.menuextra.battery
ShowPercent -string "NO"
```

```
defaults write com.apple.menuextra.battery
ShowTime -string "YES"
```

Menu bar: hide the Time Machine and Volume icons

```
defaults write com.apple.systemuiserver
menuExtras -array "/System/Library/CoreServices/
Menu Extras/Bluetooth.menu" "/System/Library/
CoreServices/Menu Extras/AirPort.menu" "/System/
Library/CoreServices/Menu Extras/Battery.menu" "/
System/Library/CoreServices/Menu Extras/Clock.
menu"
```

Always show Scrollbars

```
defaults write NSGlobalDomain AppleShowScrollBars
-string "Always"
```

Disable opening and closing window animations

```
defaults write NSGlobalDomain
NSAutomaticWindowAnimationsEnabled -bool false
```

Increase window resize speed for Cocoa applications

```
defaults write NSGlobalDomain NSWindowResizeTime
-float 0.001
```

Expand Save panel by default

```
defaults write NSGlobalDomain
NSNavPanelExpandedStateForSaveMode -bool true
```

Expand Print panel by default

```
defaults write NSGlobalDomain
PMPrintingExpandedStateForPrint -bool true
```

Disable the "Are you sure you want to open this application?" dialog

```
defaults write com.apple.LaunchServices
LSQuarantine -bool false
```

Display ASCII control characters using caret notation in standard text views

```
defaults write NSGlobalDomain
NSTextShowsControlCharacters -bool true
```

...cont'd

Disable Resume system-wide

```
defaults write NSGlobalDomain
NSQuitAlwaysKeepsWindows -bool false
```

Disable Automatic Termination of Inactive Apps

```
defaults write NSGlobalDomain
NSDisableAutomaticTermination -bool true
```

Trackpad: enable tap to Click for this user and for the Login screen

```
defaults write com.apple.driver.
AppleBluetoothMultitouch.trackpad Clicking -bool
true
```

```
defaults -currentHost write NSGlobalDomain com.
apple.mouse.tapBehavior -int 1
```

```
defaults write NSGlobalDomain com.apple.mouse.
tapBehavior -int 1
```

Trackpad: map bottom right corner to right-click

```
defaults write com.apple.driver.
AppleBluetoothMultitouch.trackpad
TrackpadCornerSecondaryClick -int 2
```

```
defaults write com.apple.driver.
AppleBluetoothMultitouch.trackpad
TrackpadRightClick -bool true
```

```
defaults -currentHost write NSGlobalDomain com.
apple.trackpad.trackpadCornerClickBehavior -int 1
```

```
defaults -currentHost write NSGlobalDomain com.
apple.trackpad.enableSecondaryClick -bool true
```

Trackpad: swipe between pages with three fingers

```
defaults write NSGlobalDomain
AppleEnableSwipeNavigateWithScrolls -bool true
```

```
defaults -currentHost write NSGlobalDomain com.
apple.trackpad.threeFingerHorizSwipeGesture -int 1
```

```
defaults write com.apple.driver.
AppleBluetoothMultitouch.trackpad
TrackpadThreeFingerHorizSwipeGesture -int 1
```

Disable "natural" (Lion-style) scrolling

Some people like this but it's the first thing I switch off. It feels anything but natural!

```
defaults write NSGlobalDomain com.apple.
swipescrolldirection -bool false
```

Increase sound quality for Bluetooth headphones/headsets

```
defaults write com.apple.BluetoothAudioAgent
"Apple Bitpool Min (editable)" -int 40
```

Enable full keyboard access for all controls

```
defaults write NSGlobalDomain AppleKeyboardUIMode
-int 3
```

Disable press-and-hold for keys in favor of key repeat

```
defaults write NSGlobalDomain
ApplePressAndHoldEnabled -bool false
```

Set a fast keyboard repeat rate

```
defaults write NSGlobalDomain KeyRepeat -int 0
```

Set language and text formats

If you are in the US, replace "EUR" with "USD", "Centimeters" with "Inches", and "true" with "false".

```
defaults write NSGlobalDomain AppleLanguages
-array "en" "nl"
```

```
defaults write NSGlobalDomain AppleLocale
-string "en_GB@currency=EUR"
```

```
defaults write NSGlobalDomain
AppleMeasurementUnits -string "Centimeters"
```

```
defaults write NSGlobalDomain AppleMetricUnits
-bool true
```

...cont'd

Disable Auto-correct

```
defaults write NSGlobalDomain
NSAutomaticSpellingCorrectionEnabled -bool false
```

Kill a Process

Sometimes you just need a process to stop running. If you want to kill it in Terminal without using Activity Monitor, find the process ID (in Activity Monitor) and then use the following command.

```
kill PID 478
```

Let Terminal Talk

You can get Terminal to speak anything back to you using the voice engine. Replace "hello" with anything you want.

```
say hello
```

Make Hidden Applications icons transparent

If you hide a lot of applications, you can make their icons transparent in the dock.

```
defaults write com.apple.Dock showhidden -bool
YES
```

```
killall Dock
```

Make the Dock spring-loaded

Makes the dock spring-loaded so you can open files or windows from within the dock.

```
defaults write com.apple.dock enable-spring-load-
actions-on-all-items -boolean YES
```

Recent Applications Stack

This command creates a new stack in your dock so you can view the recently-used Applications.

```
defaults write com.apple.dock persistent-others
-array-add '{ "tile-data" = { "list-type" = 1;
}; "tile-type" = "recents-tile"; }'
```

Pin Dock to the right

```
defaults write com.apple.dock pinning -string
"start"
```

Pin Dock to the left

```
defaults write com.apple.dock pinning -string
"end"
```

Pin Dock to the center (back to the way it was)

```
defaults write com.apple.dock pinning -string
"middle"
```

Quick Look a file

This command lets you Quick Look a file in Terminal. First, you need to change the folder by using the "cd" command and then enter the folder you want. To enable this command to work you need to type the file name exactly.

```
qlmanage -p "Jaguar Aqua Graphite.jpg"
```

Disable the Spotlight icon

This command removes the spotlight icon. Type 755 to re-enable it, instead of 0.

```
sudo chmod 0 /System/Library/CoreServices/
Spotlight.app
```

```
killall Spotlight
```

Remove the stripes in List View

A simple hack that removes the alternating stripes in list view in finder.

```
defaults write com.apple.finder FXListViewStripes
-bool FALSE
```

```
killall Finder
```

Change the Menu Bar to white

If you don't like the transparent menu bar you can change it so that it appears white. This requires a password and you will need to restart your Mac.

...cont'd

```
sudo defaults write /System/Library/
LaunchDaemons/com.apple.WindowServer
'EnvironmentVariables' -dict 'CI_NO_BACKGROUND_
IMAGE' 1
```

Change the Menu Bar to gray

If you don't like the white version of the menu bar you can change it so that it appears gray.

```
sudo defaults write /System/Library/
LaunchDaemons/com.apple.WindowServer
'EnvironmentVariables' -dict 'CI_NO_BACKGROUND_
IMAGE' 0
```

Revert the Menu Bar back to default

If you prefer the transparent menu bar and you want it back, type the following into Terminal.

```
sudo defaults delete /System/Library/
LaunchDaemons/com.apple.WindowServer
'EnvironmentVariables'
```

Set the expanded Print dialog as default

If you want access to a lot of the extra print menus by default you can use the following command to enable you to do this. Requires a restart.

```
defaults write -g PMPrintingExpandedStateForPrint
-bool TRUE
```

Set the expanded Save dialog as default

Similar to the print dialogue this sets the save dialogue to the expanded view by default. This requires a restart.

```
defaults write -g
NSNavPanelExpandedStateForSaveMode -bool TRUE
```

Set the Screen saver as the wallpaper

This command sets the currently-selected screen saver as the desktop background.

```
/System/Library/Frameworks/ScreenSaver.framework/
Resources/ScreenSaverEngine.app/Contents/MacOS/
ScreenSaverEngine -background
```

Show Hidden Files in Finder

A lot of the files in Finder are hidden. If you want to take a look at how many there are and what they are you can show them within Finder. Be careful, as these files are needed by the system. Repeat the command with "false" to revert.

```
defaults write com.apple.finder AppleShowAllFiles
TRUE
```

Skip Disk Image verification

If you want to save some time you can skip the disk image verification for a disk image.

```
com.apple.frameworks.diskimages skip-verify TRUE
```

Show Subfolders in graphical format in Terminal

This is a very cool hack that enables you to show an ASCII graphical view of sub folders. Use the cd command to change to a directory, otherwise the command will list every folder.

```
ls -R | grep ":$" | sed -e 's/:$//' -e 's/[^-]
[^\/]*\//--/g' -e 's/^/ /' -e 's/-/|/'
```

Speed up Dialog boxes

Most dialogue boxes have an animation effect that looks cool. If you want to speed this up you can change the speed at which it renders so it appears almost instantly. The default is 0.2.

```
defaults write NSGlobalDomain NSWindowResizeTime
0.01
```

Restart Mac OS X

```
shutdown - r now
```

Shutdown Mac OS X

```
shutdown now
```

Get overview of current Power Management Settings

```
pmset -g
```

Put Display to sleep after 15 minutes of inactivity

```
sudo pmset displaysleep 15
```

...cont'd

Put Computer to sleep after 30 minutes of inactivity

```
sudo pmset sleep 30
```

Permanently disable Dock icon bouncing

```
$ defaults write com.apple.dock no-bouncing
-bool TRUE
```

```
$ killall Dock
```

Disable Dashboard (don't forget to drag the Dashboard Dock icon off the Dock too)

```
defaults write com.apple.dashboard mcx-disabled
-boolean YES
```

```
killall Dock
```

Enable Dashboard

```
defaults write com.apple.dashboard mcx-disabled
-boolean NO
```

```
killall Dock
```

Force the Finder to show hidden files

This is useful for Web Developers who need to edit .htaccess files, for example.

```
defaults write com.apple.finder AppleShowAllFiles
TRUE
```

Force the Finder to hide hidden files

Require password immediately after sleep or screen saver begins.

```
defaults write com.apple.screensaver
askForPassword -int 1
```

```
defaults write com.apple.screensaver
askForPasswordDelay -int 0
```

Save Screenshots to the Desktop

```
defaults write com.apple.screencapture location
-string "$HOME/Desktop"
```

Disable shadow in Screenshots

```
defaults write com.apple.screencapture disable-
shadow -bool true
```

Enable subpixel font rendering on non-Apple LCDs

```
defaults write NSGlobalDomain AppleFontSmoothing
-int 2
```

Finder: allow quitting via ⌘ + Q; doing so will also hide desktop icons

```
defaults write com.apple.finder QuitMenuItem
-bool true
```

Finder: disable window animations and Get Info animations

```
defaults write com.apple.finder
DisableAllAnimations -bool true
```

Show icons for hard drives, servers, and removable media on the desktop

```
defaults write com.apple.finder
ShowExternalHardDrivesOnDesktop -bool true

defaults write com.apple.finder
ShowHardDrivesOnDesktop -bool true

defaults write com.apple.finder
ShowMountedServersOnDesktop -bool true

defaults write com.apple.finder
ShowRemovableMediaOnDesktop -bool true
```

Finder: show hidden files by default

```
defaults write com.apple.Finder AppleShowAllFiles
-bool true
```

Finder: show all filename extensions

```
defaults write NSGlobalDomain
AppleShowAllExtensions -bool true
```

...cont'd

Finder: show status bar

```
defaults write com.apple.finder ShowStatusBar
-bool true
```

Finder: allow text selection in Quick Look

```
defaults write com.apple.finder
QLEnableTextSelection -bool true
```

Display full POSIX path as Finder window title

```
defaults write com.apple.finder
FXShowPosixPathInTitle -bool true
```

Disable the warning when changing a file extension

```
defaults write com.apple.finder
FXEnableExtensionChangeWarning -bool false
```

Avoid creating .DS_Store files on network volumes

```
defaults write com.apple.desktopservices
DSDontWriteNetworkStores -bool true
```

Automatically open a new Finder window when a volume is mounted

```
defaults write com.apple.frameworks.diskimages
auto-open-ro-root -bool true
```

```
defaults write com.apple.frameworks.diskimages
auto-open-rw-root -bool true
```

```
defaults write com.apple.finder
OpenWindowForNewRemovableDisk -bool true
```

Show item info below icons on the desktop and in other icon views

```
/usr/libexec/PlistBuddy -c "Set :DesktopViewS
ettings:IconViewSettings:showItemInfo true" ~/
Library/Preferences/com.apple.finder.plist
```

```
/usr/libexec/PlistBuddy -c "Set :FK_StandardVie
wSettings:IconViewSettings:showItemInfo true" ~/
Library/Preferences/com.apple.finder.plist
```

```
/usr/libexec/PlistBuddy -c "Set :StandardViewS
ettings:IconViewSettings:showItemInfo true" ~/
Library/Preferences/com.apple.finder.plist
```

Enable snap-to-grid for icons on the desktop and in other icon views

```
/usr/libexec/PlistBuddy -c "Set :DesktopViewSett
ings:IconViewSettings:arrangeBy grid" ~/Library/
Preferences/com.apple.finder.plist
```

```
/usr/libexec/PlistBuddy -c "Set :FK_StandardVi
ewSettings:IconViewSettings:arrangeBy grid" ~/
Library/Preferences/com.apple.finder.plist
```

```
/usr/libexec/PlistBuddy -c "Set :StandardViewSet
tings:IconViewSettings:arrangeBy grid" ~/Library/
Preferences/com.apple.finder.plist
```

Increase grid spacing for icons on the desktop and in other icon views

```
/usr/libexec/PlistBuddy -c "Set :DesktopViewSett
ings:IconViewSettings:gridSpacing 100" ~/Library/
Preferences/com.apple.finder.plist
```

```
/usr/libexec/PlistBuddy -c "Set :FK_StandardVi
ewSettings:IconViewSettings:gridSpacing 100" ~/
Library/Preferences/com.apple.finder.plist
```

```
/usr/libexec/PlistBuddy -c "Set :StandardViewSett
ings:IconViewSettings:gridSpacing 100" ~/Library/
Preferences/com.apple.finder.plist
```

Increase the size of icons on the desktop and in other icon views

```
/usr/libexec/PlistBuddy -c "Set :DesktopViewSe
ttings:IconViewSettings:iconSize 80" ~/Library/
Preferences/com.apple.finder.plist
```

```
/usr/libexec/PlistBuddy -c "Set :FK_StandardView
Settings:IconViewSettings:iconSize 80" ~/Library/
Preferences/com.apple.finder.plist
```

...cont'd

```
/usr/libexec/PlistBuddy -c "Set :StandardViewSe
ttings:IconViewSettings:iconSize 80" ~/Library/
Preferences/com.apple.finder.plist
```

Disable the warning before emptying the Trash

```
defaults write com.apple.finder WarnOnEmptyTrash
-bool false
```

Empty Trash securely by default

```
defaults write com.apple.finder EmptyTrashSecurely
-bool true
```

Show the ~/Library folder

```
chflags nohidden ~/Library
```

Remove Dropbox's green checkmark icons in Finder

```
file=/Applications/Dropbox.app/Contents/Resources/
check.icns

[ -e "$file" ] && mv -f "$file" "$file.bak"

unset file
```

Enable highlight hover effect for the grid view of a stack (Dock)

```
defaults write com.apple.dock mouse-over-hilte-
stack -bool true
```

Set the icon size of Dock items to 36 pixels

```
defaults write com.apple.dock tilesize -int 36
```

Enable spring loading for all Dock items

```
defaults write com.apple.dock enable-spring-load-
actions-on-all-items -bool true
```

Show indicator lights for open applications in the Dock

```
defaults write com.apple.dock show-process-
indicators -bool true
```

Don't animate opening applications from the Dock

```
defaults write com.apple.dock launchanim -bool
false
```

Speed up Mission Control animations

```
defaults write com.apple.dock expose-animation-
duration -float 0.1
```

Top left screen corner → Mission Control

```
defaults write com.apple.dock wvous-tl-corner
-int 2
```

```
defaults write com.apple.dock wvous-tl-modifier
-int 0
```

Top right screen corner → Desktop

```
defaults write com.apple.dock wvous-tr-corner
-int 4
```

```
defaults write com.apple.dock wvous-tr-modifier
-int 0
```

Bottom left screen corner → Start screen saver

```
defaults write com.apple.dock wvous-bl-corner
-int 5
```

```
defaults write com.apple.dock wvous-bl-modifier
-int 0
```

Remove the auto-hiding Dock delay

```
defaults write com.apple.Dock autohide-delay
-float 0
```

Remove the animation when hiding/showing the Dock

```
defaults write com.apple.dock autohide-time-
modifier -float 0
```

```
#defaults write com.apple.dock no-glass -bool
true
```

Automatically hide and show the Dock

```
defaults write com.apple.dock autohide -bool
true
```

Make Dock icons of hidden applications translucent

```
defaults write com.apple.dock showhidden -bool
true
```

Reset Launchpad

```
find ~/Library/Application\ Support/Dock -name
"*.db" -maxdepth 1 -delete
```

Add a spacer to the left side of the Dock (where the applications are)

```
#defaults write com.apple.dock persistent-apps
-array-add '{tile-data={}; tile-type="spacer-
tile";}'
```

Add a spacer to the right side of the Dock (where the Trash is)

```
#defaults write com.apple.dock persistent-others
-array-add '{tile-data={}; tile-type="spacer-
tile";}'
```

Add a context menu item for showing the Web Inspector in web views

```
defaults write NSGlobalDomain
WebKitDeveloperExtras -bool true
```

Enable Dashboard dev mode (allows keeping widgets on the desktop)

```
defaults write com.apple.dashboard devmode -bool
true
```

Disable smart quotes as it's annoying for code tweets

```
defaults write com.twitter.twitter-mac
AutomaticQuoteSubstitutionEnabled -bool false
```

Show the app window when clicking the menu icon

```
defaults write com.twitter.twitter-mac
MenuItemBehavior -int 1
```

Enable the hidden "Develop" menu

```
defaults write com.twitter.twitter-mac
ShowDevelopMenu -bool true
```

Hide the app in the background if it's not the front-most window

This is a very useful command for anyone who does a lot of fiddling and needs to quit Finder.

```
defaults write com.apple.finder QuitMenuItem
-bool YES
```

```
killall Finder
```

App-specific Commands

Web inspector for Safari

This is a very detailed web inspector that enables you to find out specific information about a page. It is accessible through the debug menu but this enables you to use it without. You can access it quickly through right-click.

```
defaults write com.apple.Safari
WebKitDeveloperExtras -bool true
```

See current path of Finder window

```
defaults write com.apple.finder _
FXShowPosixPathInTitle -bool YES
```

Enable Time Machine on unsupported drives

This hack enables Time Machine to work on unsupported drives such as a NAS. Use with caution as it is unsupported.

```
defaults write com.apple.systempreferences
TMShowUnsupportedNetworkVolumes 1
```

Increase Time Machine backups

To change to half-hourly backups use this hack.

```
sudo defaults write /System/Library/
LaunchDaemons/com.apple.backupd-auto
StartInterval -int 1800
```

Enable the debug menu in iCal

```
defaults write com.apple.iCal IncludeDebugMenu
-bool true
```

```
hash tmutil &> /dev/null && sudo tmutil
disablelocal
```

Force Mail to display in plain text

```
defaults write com.apple.mail PreferPlainText
-bool TRUE
```

Disable Tooltips in Safari

This quick hack for Safari removes the tooltips you get when you hover over certain elements.

```
defaults write com.apple.Safari
WebKitShowsURLsInToolTips 0
```

Change the loading bar in Safari to a pie chart

This changes the blue bar that goes across the address bar into a small blue pie chart. Insert "false" instead of "true" to reverse.

```
defaults write com.apple.Safari
DebugUsePieProgressIndicator -bool true
```

Enable debug menu in Safari

Adding debug menus to programs is great, as you can access a whole range of features. This one is for Safari.

```
defaults write com.apple.Safari IncludeDebugMenu 1
```

Set the history limit in Safari to a number of items

```
defaults write com.apple.Safari
WebKitHistoryItemLimit 2000
```

Set the history limit in Safari to a number of days

```
defaults write com.apple.Safari
WebKitHistoryAgeInDaysLimit 30
```

Disable Safari's thumbnail cache for history and top sites

```
defaults write com.apple.Safari
DebugSnapshotsUpdatePolicy -int 2
```

```
defaults write com.apple.Safari
IncludeInternalDebugMenu -bool true
```

Make Safari's search banners default to "contains" instead of "starts with"

```
defaults write com.apple.Safari
FindOnPageMatchesWordStartsOnly -bool false
```

Remove unwanted icons from Safari's bookmarks bar

```
defaults write com.apple.Safari
ProxiesInBookmarksBar "()"
```

...cont'd

Change The Arrows In iTunes

Normally the arrows in iTunes link to the music store. Adding this command enables you to search your library. You need to click on the song first for the arrows to appear.

```
defaults write com.apple.iTunes invertStoreLinks
-bool YES
```

Change iTunes link behavior to point at local iTunes Library instead of iTunes Store

```
defaults write com.apple.iTunes invertStoreLinks
-bool true
```

```
defaults write com.apple.iTunes invertStoreLinks
-bool YES
```

Disable the iTunes arrow links completely

```
defaults write com.apple.iTunes show-store-arrow-
links -bool false
```

Enable iTunes track notifications in the Dock

```
defaults write com.apple.dock itunes-notifications
-bool true
```

Make ⌘ + F focus the search input in iTunes

```
defaults write com.apple.iTunes
NSUserKeyEquivalents -dict-add "Target Search
Field" "@F"
```

Sync to Dropbox from anywhere in your home folder

Using this terminal command you can create symbolic links to folders you want to sync within Dropbox.

```
(replace username, foldername, and path/to/
dropbox with your own values):
```

```
ln -s /Users/username/Documents/foldername /
Users/path/to/dropbox/Files/
```

Disable send and reply animations in Mail.app

```
defaults write com.apple.Mail
DisableReplyAnimations -bool true
```

```
defaults write com.apple.Mail
DisableSendAnimations -bool true
```

Copy email addresses as "johndoe@mac.com" instead of John Doe <johndoe@mac.com> in Mail.app

```
defaults write com.apple.mail
AddressesIncludeNameOnPasteboard -bool false
```

Enable the debug menu in Disk Utility

```
defaults write com.apple.DiskUtility
DUDebugMenuEnabled -bool true
```

Prevent Time Machine from prompting to use new hard drives as backup volume

```
defaults write com.apple.TimeMachine
DoNotOfferNewDisksForBackup -bool true
```

Enable the debug menu in Address Book

```
defaults write com.apple.addressbook
ABShowDebugMenu -bool true
```

Entertainment

Play Star Wars Episode IV

Using a simple Telnet address your Terminal will connect in and play Star Wars Episode IV in ASCII format!

telnet towel.blinkenlights.nl

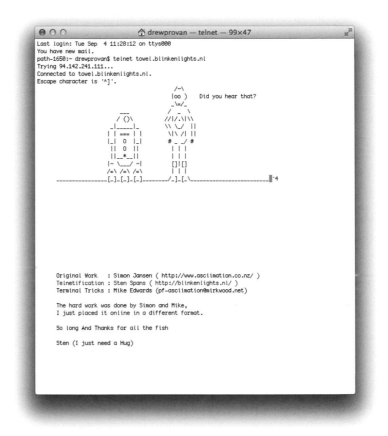

Tetris and Pong

Open Terminal, type

emacs

click enter

Press ESC + X at the same time

Type

tetris

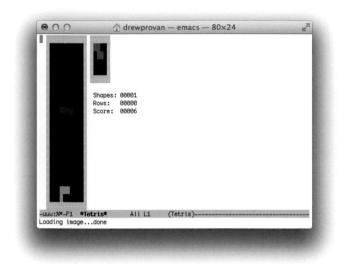

or

pong

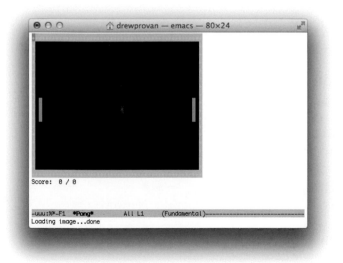

Use the arrow keys to move and rotate the blocks, and press the space to make the blocks fall.

Networking and Internet

Ping a host to see whether it's available

```
ping -o leftcolumn.net
```

Troubleshoot routing problems to a host using traceroute

```
traceroute leftcolumn.net
```

Check whether a host is running an HTTP server (i.e. check that a Web Site is available)

```
curl -I www.leftcolumn.net | head -n 1
```

Who is logged in to your Mac?

```
w
```

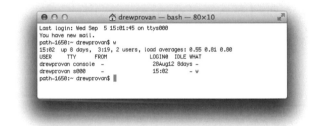

Show routing table

```
netstat -r
```

Show active network connections

```
netstat -an
```

Show network statistics

```
netstat -s
```

Restart Bonjour

Useful when a Mac 'disappears' from the Network.

```
sudo launchctl unload /System/Library/
LaunchDaemons/com.apple.mDNSResponder.plist
```

```
sudo launchctl load /System/Library/
LaunchDaemons/com.apple.mDNSResponder.plist
```

11 Tips & Tricks for Common Apps

Most OS X apps work fine straight out of the box but you can improve productivity hugely by exploring the options available for these apps. In this section we will look at the common built-in OS X apps such as Mail, iTunes, iPhoto, Safari, Reminders, and others.

Make Mail work for You!

Apple's mail program is a great Mail client but it is set up fairly simply by default. There are several things you can modify to make it more powerful:

- Customize the Toolbar

- Use signatures for your accounts

- Set up email rules to filter items

- Use Smart Mailboxes to store specific types of email

Customize the Toolbar

There are more items you can add to the Toolbar but these are not shown by default because many people would not want to use them. To beef up the Toolbar:

1 Open Mail, right-click on the Toolbar and select **Customize Toolbar...** Drag the items you want to add to the Toolbar and click **Done**

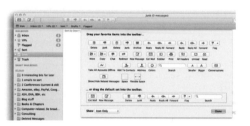

Use signatures

 These are small pieces of text that appear in your emails saving you having to type out your contact details, or paste in your company logo each time. Once you have set up a few signatures (personal, work-related, etc) you can drag-and-drop these onto the accounts that you want associated with each type of signature:

1 Go to **Mail > Preferences > Signatures**

2 Click the **+** symbol and **add your signature**

3 **Drag** the signature to each account with which you want to use that signature

Hot tip

Using Mail signatures makes a more professional impression, especially if you are using Mail for business purposes.

Use Rules!

Rules can streamline your email. By telling Mail what you want to do with incoming email you can save yourself the hassle of filing each one individually. For example, emails from your friends can be targeted to a Personal email folder:

1 Go to **Mail > Preferences > Rules**

Smart Mailboxes

These are like smart playlists in iTunes where you can set up a smart mailbox to store, for example, all emails containing attachments, or emails containing only presentation files created within the last 12 months, and so on.

Safari Tips

Quickly enable Private Browsing

Private browsing lets you view websites without leaving any trace of your visit. There will be no temporary cache files and your history will not show where you've been. This is useful if you are using a Mac other than your own:

 Go to **Safari > Private Browsing** (slow method, gets tedious)

2 Speed up Private Browsing by creating a keyboard shortcut: Go to **System Preferences > Keyboard > Keyboard Shortcuts**

3 Click **Application Shortcuts**

4 Click the **+** symbol and choose **Safari** and type **Private Browsing**

5 Choose a sequence of key commands, e.g. ⌘ **+ Shift + P**

![Keyboard preferences window showing Keyboard Shortcuts tab with Application Shortcuts selected and Private Browsing shortcut highlighted]

Keyboard

Keyboard | Keyboard Shortcuts

To change a shortcut, double-click the shortcut and hold down the new keys.

- Launchpad & Dock
- Mission Control
- Keyboard & Text...
- Screen Shots
- Services
- Spotlight
- Accessibility
- Application Shor...

▼ All Applications
☑ Show Help menu   ⇧⌘/
▼ Safari
    Private Browsing   ⇧⌘P

Full Keyboard Access: In windows and dialogs, press Tab to move keyboard focus between:
- ◉ Text boxes and lists only
- ○ All controls

Press Control+F7 to change this setting.

Set Up Bluetooth Keyboard...   ⑦

Quickly bring up Safari Reader
Reader is a place to store web pages for reading offline, and for those you want to have ready to read rather than hunt through bookmarks.

Activate Reader quickly by clicking ⌘ **+ Shift + R.**

Make new Safari tabs immediately active
Hold down Cmd + Shift while clicking a link. This brings up a new tab that becomes active straight away.

Merge windows into tabs
Sometimes you have numerous Safari windows scattered across your screen. You can merge these into one Safari window with all the pages now converted to separate tabs:

   Go to **Safari > Window > Merge All Windows**

Instantly tidier!

Getting more out of Preview

Merge two or more PDFs into one

Merging PDF files is useful but not intuitive. You can drag one PDF onto another which is open in Preview but when you close the PDF you find they have not merged into one. Here's how to do it:

1 **Open the first PDF** in Preview

2 Make sure you can see the **thumbnails** on the left hand side

3 **Drag the second PDF** onto the thumbnail view of the first PDF but make sure you drag it **above the line**. If you drag it below the line it will appear to be added to the first PDF but it will not be saved. If you're sure you have added it above the line, close the PDF and reopen it to check both documents have been merged into one PDF

4 The title will still be that of the original PDF so you may want to **rename** it

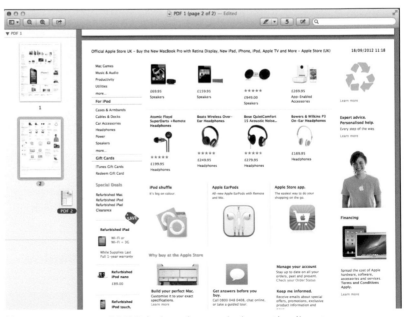

Here you can see PDF 2 being dragged above the line to merge.

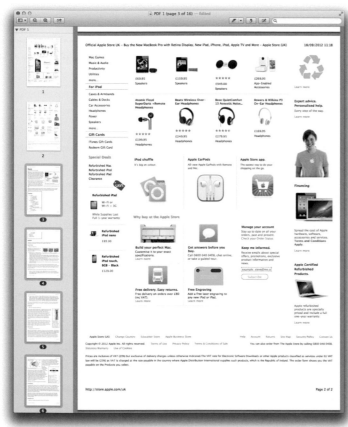

Here is the resulting merged PDF document.

Reduce PDF file size

PDF files containing lots of images can be huge. It is easy to reduce the file size:

1 **Open the PDF** to be reduced

2 Go to **Export > Quartz Filter: Reduce File Size**

3 Click **Save**

4 The PDF will now be very much smaller than before

iPhoto

Stop iPhoto opening when you connect a camera

 Open **iPhoto > Preferences** and under the General tab click the menu **Connecting camera opens:** make sure it says **No application**

 iPhoto should no longer launch when you plug in your camera, iPhone or other device containing photos

Move your iPhoto library to another drive

 Locate your iPhoto library (in your Pictures folder) and copy to your drive of choice

 Double-click the library file and iPhoto will remember where it is

Set up multiple iPhoto libraries
You can add two or more additional libraries by holding down the Option key when you launch iPhoto.

Location-based Reminders

Apple has recently introduced reminders that pop up when you are in a specific location. This was already a feature of iOS devices like iPhone and iPad but is now built into the Reminders app on the Mac.

Set up a location-based reminder

1 Open the Reminders app

2 **Select a reminder** or create a new one

3 To the right of the reminder title you will see a circle with "**I**" (information)

4 Click this and select **At a Location**

5 **Enter the zip code or location details**

6 When Geotagging determines you are near that location the reminder will pop up!

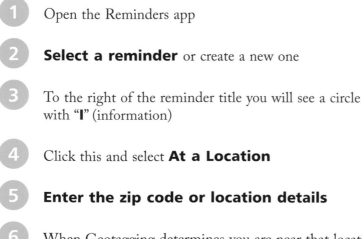

iTunes Tips

Backup your iTunes library

Hard drives often fail so it is worth backing up your entire music library in the event of a hard drive disaster:

1 Go to **~/Music/iTunes/iTunes Music**

2 **Drag this file to the backup drive**

3 Your music and other media will be copied across to the backup drive

Moving your iTunes library

If you have a lot of music on your Mac you may want to move the music folder to another location. iTunes will become confused since it will not know where the music folder has moved to so you need to tell it the location of the Music Library:

1 Locate your iTunes files by going to **~/Music/iTunes/ iTunes Music**

2 Drag this folder to its new location

3 Open iTunes and go to **iTunes > Preferences > Advanced**. Under **iTunes Media Folder Location**

you will see the path of your media folder. To let iTunes know the new location, click **Change...** and navigate to where the media folder is located

4 Then click **Open**

Create additional iTunes libraries

1 Start iTunes while holding down **Option**

2 **Create a new library** (similar to iPhoto, *see Page 198*)

Use iSight Camera for Notes

If you jot things down on post-it notes or scraps of paper you may lose them somewhere. Why not try photographing the bit of paper and uploading to Evernote or dropping into Apple Notes?

Taking a picture

1 Launch **Photo Booth**

2 Hold your note up so the iSight camera can see it and **take a picture**

3 **Drag to the desktop**

4 Or use a smartphone, or iPad to take a picture and move it to the desktop so you can access it

5 Open **Notes** and drop the picture onto it (or drop it onto **Evernote** where the OCR software will actually make the text searchable so you can find it easily later)

6 Alternatively, drop it into Word or some other app

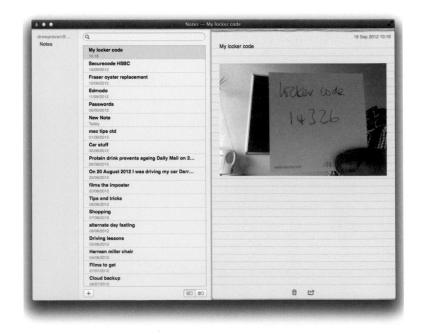

Convert DVDs with Handbrake

You can use your Mac to put movies onto your iPhone, iPad, iPod Touch, Apple TV and other devices very easily. This works with standard DVDs, but not Blu-Ray DVDs:

1 **Download Handbrake** (free) from *http://handbrake.fr*

2 Install and launch the app

3 Put the DVD you want to convert into the CD/DVD slot of your Mac and Handbrake will ask you choose the **Source**

4 Choose the DVD and Handbrake will analyze the files on the DVD and will configure itself so that the **largest file** (the film) will be at the top of the drop-down menu

5 Choose the **output format** and click **Convert**

6 Handbrake will convert the film and save to the desktop

7 **Drop onto iTunes** or wherever you want to store it

8 **Sync** with your mobile device

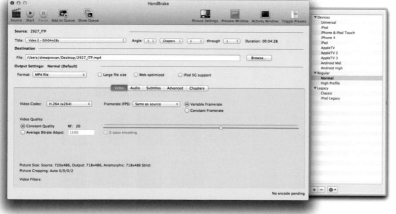

Image Capture App

Most people don't use Image Capture much. This simple app will mount your camera, iPhone, iPad or any other device with images or videos and display these in its window.

Viewing your media in Image Capture
You can delete photos from your iOS device, drag them to the desktop or copy the iPhone's entire camera roll to a folder for editing or viewing:

Hot tip

You can tell Image Capture never to open when a camera or other device is connected.

1 **Attach** your camera or iOS device to your Mac

2 Open **Image Capture**

3 Your photos (and videos if you have any) should all display in the window

4 You may need to **click the black triangle** on the left to select your device, especially if you have more than one device plugged into your Mac

5 To delete an image, click it to select it then click the **Delete** icon at the bottom of the Image Capture window

Explore your iOS Device

iOS devices like iPhones, iPads, and iPod Touches are essentially hard drives which can be plugged into a Mac or PC and mounted. This lets you view all the files on the device.

The iExplorer app works with both Mac OS X and PC. It lets you plug in your iOS device and your folders and files show up ready for deleting or copying to the Desktop. You can even listen to voicemails and download your text messages as a PDF!

Warning: be very careful when it comes to deleting files from your device. It may never work again if you delete a critical file. It is probably wisest simply to use the app to view your photos and videos.

1. **Download iExplorer 3** from *http://www.macroplant. com/iexplorer/*

2. **Plug in your iPhone** or other iOS device

3. Launch iExplorer 3

4. You will see the directory structure listing everything on your iPhone or iOS device including music, videos, books, text messages, voicemails, etc.

5. **Click the black triangles** to view files within folders

Be careful if you decide to delete files from your iPhone or other device. You make cause the device to stop working completely.

Annotate PDFs with Skitch

Annotating PDFs is not only for the business world. The free app Skitch (*http://skitch.com*, now owned by Evernote) lets you drop images or PDFs onto the app and you can add text, shapes and do other cool things.

Another cool thing about Skitch is that it's totally free!

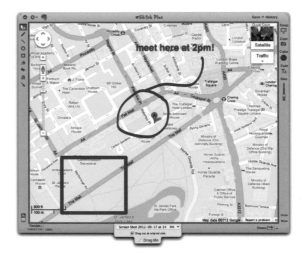

Here I have opened a PDF file (Skitch restricts you to the first page only) and you can see the number of different save formats Skitch has.

12 Keeping your Mac Secure

Although there are few Mac-specific viruses, you need to be security conscious even on a Mac. Here we will explore various ways of keeping your information away from prying eyes, and also look at methods for preventing cyber attacks.

FileVault

This is one of OS X's built-in security features. FileVault encrypts all the files in your home folder using 128 bit encryption. Once you activate FileVault *you will not be able to open any of your files or folders unless you enter the correct password*. If your Mac is stolen, the thief could access personal data on your Mac but if you have turned on FileVault, encrypted files will not be readable without the required password or security key.

Setting up FileVault

 Go to **System Preferences > Security & Privacy** and click FileVault

2 Click the **lock** icon on the lower left of the **Security & Privacy window** and enter your administrator **password**

3 **Turn on FileVault**

4 You will then see a security key which can be used to unlock your disk if you forget your password

5 Click **Continue** and choose whether to let Apple store your recovery key

6 Click **Continue**

7 **Restart** your Mac and start the encryption process

Disable Automatic Login

If you are the sole user of your Mac you may have it configured such that when you switch on the Mac it automatically boots up and takes you straight to the desktop. This may save you a few seconds but it means that if anyone steals your Mac they can have easy access to all your files and folders. It is a wise precaution to disable automatic login, which means that when you start your Mac you're taken to the login screen which will show your account, a guest account and the accounts of any other users configured to use that Mac. Each person will have to log in using their own password. This stops prying eyes viewing your files.

Disable automatic login

1 Go to **System Preferences > Security & Privacy**

2 Click the **lock** at the bottom left of the window to make changes and enter your **password**

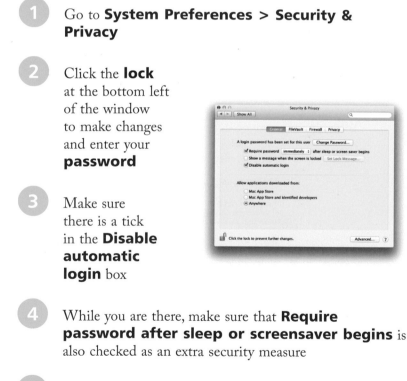

3 Make sure there is a tick in the **Disable automatic login** box

4 While you are there, make sure that **Require password after sleep or screensaver begins** is also checked as an extra security measure

5 Finally, if you intend to install software from third parties and elsewhere rather than only from the Mac App Store or identified developers, click the **Anywhere** radio button

6 Click the lock to prevent further changes and close the window

Secure Empty Trash

Normally when you empty the Trash the file or folder disappears which makes you think the file has been destroyed. In fact, all that has happened is that the Mac has removed that file's name from your computer but the file actually still remains on the hard drive and could be accessed if somebody wanted to recover your data.

If you really want to remove the file *completely* along with its contents you need to empty the trash securely. Emptying the trash securely forces the Mac to overwrite your data with random system-generated data which makes it impossible to recover the file. *Note of caution*: only use secure emptying if you're absolutely sure you will never want to recover the data.

Beware

Once you use Secure Empty Trash you cannot recover the file!

Empty Trash securely

1 Place your files or folders into the Trash

2 Go to **Finder > Secure Empty Trash**

3 Your file will now be deleted securely

About Finder	
Preferences...	⌘,
Empty Trash	⇧⌘⌫
Secure Empty Trash	
Services	▶
Hide Finder	⌘H
Hide Others	⌥⌘H
Show All	

If you place large amounts of data in the Trash the Secure Empty Trash procedure may take a long time because the system has to write random data to such a large file.

Empty Trash securely by default

You can also use Secure Empty Trash by default by using Terminal and typing:

```
defaults write com.apple.finder EmptyTrashSecurely
-bool true
```

Activate OS X Firewall

Firewalls can be either software or hardware security barriers that monitor incoming and outgoing network traffic on your Mac. Firewalls determine whether either incoming or outgoing traffic should be allowed.

Most of us are using wireless routers which have firewalls built into them so it is a moot point as to whether you need to activate the Mac OS X-based firewall as well as your router's firewall. Personally, I use the firewall in my router and have the firewall in Mac OS X switched off.

Switch on Mac OS X Firewall

1 Go to **System References > Security & Privacy**

2 Click the **Firewall** tab

3 Click the **lock** at the bottom left of the window to make changes and enter password

4 Click **Turn On Firewall**

5 You can review the options available by clicking the **Firewall Options...** button (for example you can block all incoming connections, enable stealth mode, etc.)

Hot tip

One firewall is enough. If your router has one you don't need the OS X firewall as well.

Install an Antivirus App

There are very few viruses which have been designed to attack the Mac. In part, this is because PCs are much more widely used and hackers are more interested in targeting the wider PC community than the more niche-based Mac OS X community. But as Macs become more popular, hackers will no doubt design viruses targeting the Mac.

There are many Mac anti-virus programs available. Some are free and others are paid. The simplest to use is the excellent ClamXav (*www.clamxav.com*). But there is also Norton AntiVirus, McAfee, VirusBarrier and a number of others.

One of the benefits of having an anti-virus program on your Mac is that if you receive an e-mail containing a virus hidden within a file, your Mac will pick this up and you will not send the virus to another user. At the moment, the chance of any PC virus doing any harm to your Mac is negligible so I would not worry if you receive a file which contains a virus.

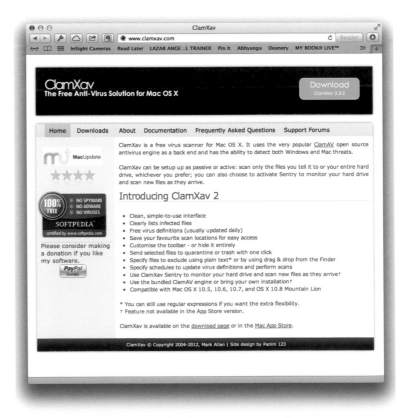

Use Keychain Access

You will find Keychain Access within your utilities folder on the Mac. The job of Keychain Access is to store web certificates, web form passwords, application passwords, private keys, and other data used to log in to applications and websites. By allowing Keychain Access to store these bits of information, it means you do not have to remember the individual passwords for the various websites and apps that you use.

Viewing Keychain Access

1 Go to **Utilities > Keychain Access** and open the app by double-clicking

2 Scroll down through the list of logins and other data

3 To view or edit a password, double-click an entry and you will see the name of the entry along with the type of entry, in this case a web form password. You will also see the account associated with the entry and the URL of the website concerned. If I want to view the password I can click the **Show password:** box. I will be prompted for my administrator password. After entering my administrator password I can view the password required to access that website

Parental Controls

If you have a family Mac and young children you will probably want to limit the things they can do on your Mac, for example install software or make changes to System Preferences. In addition, you will probably want to limit the programs they can open and the websites they can view. Mac OS X has parental controls built into the system, easily accessible via System Preferences.

Setting up Parental Controls

1 Go to **System Preferences > Parental Controls**

2 **Click the lock** at the bottom left and enter your administrator password to make changes

3 **Choose the account** for which you wish to turn on Parental Controls

4 **Click through the various tabs** on the window on the right (Apps, Web, People, Time Limits, and Other) and activate the various controls as you work through the tabs and then click the lock to prevent further changes

13 Troubleshooting the Mac

All computers go wrong from time to time and the Mac is no exception. This section looks at solving problems such as the Mac that refuses to boot up, ejecting rogue disks that won't eject, corrupt files, slow Macs and how to speed them up, and wireless networking problems.

Disk Utility

This is a great utility that comes built into Mac OS X. You will find it in the Utilities folder.

Functions of Disk Utility

1 Verifying and repairing drives

2 Erasing (formatting) drives

3 Setting up RAID storage

4 Restoring data from other drives

5 Creating disk images, mounting these, USB drives, and many other functions

Although you can buy many third-party apps at great expense to analyze and repair your drives, the inbuilt Disk Utility app is where you should start to troubleshoot your Mac and work with disks and their images.

216

Repairing permissions

If your Mac starts to misbehave, one of the first things you should do is repair the permissions using Disk Utility:

1 Open Disk Utility and select your drive from those shown in the left pane

2 Click the **First Aid** and then click **Repair Disk** Permissions

3 Restart your Mac and see if your problem is solved

Mac won't Start

Thankfully this doesn't happen often but it can be alarming when it does.

There are several types of non-starting Mac: gray screen, crashes during startup, black screen with three beeps, and others.

What you see depends on whether the startup problem is hardware or software-based.

General steps if your Mac will not start

1. **Unplug everything** you can, including USB devices, and any non-essential items leaving only keyboard and mouse connected

2. If it still fails to boot up, you may need to **remove any third-party RAM** if you have installed this (black screen with three beeps indicates faulty RAM)

3. Try to start up in **Safe Mode** (hold down Shift when the Mac starts)

4. Try **resetting the Parameter RAM (PRAM)** by holding down the **Command + Option + P + R** keys all at the same time (you will hear the chimes then the screen will go black)

5. Try to startup in **Single User Mode** – hold down **Command + S** as the Mac starts. If you do succeed and the Mac starts, you will end up with the UNIX prompt. At this point type in **/sbin/fsck -y** and the utility will report the problems

6. Try restarting from the **OS X Installer disk** if you have one (insert the DVD into the drive and hold down the C key as you start the Mac). If you are lucky enough to boot from this you can use Disk Utility and repair your drive

7. If the above measures fail you may be forced to **reinstall OS X**

Boot into Safe Mode

In addition to switching off certain features on the Mac, booting into Safe Mode has a number of very useful functions:

1 This mode forces the Mac to do a directory check on the start-up disk (as you start up into Safe Mode you will see a progress bar going along the bottom of the screen)

2 Only the absolutely essential extensions are loaded

3 All fonts are disabled apart from those in the main System Library

4 All font caches are moved to the Trash

5 All start-up items are disabled, as are login items

Using the Mountain Lion Recovery Partition

Macs are no longer supplied with installer disks but you can reinstall OS X from the Recovery Partition:

1 Start up your Mac whilst holding down ⌘ **+ R**

2 You will then see a set of OS X Utilities including: Restore From Time Machine Backup, Reinstall OS X, Get Help Online, and Disk Utility

3 To reinstall Mountain Lion choose that option

Hot tip

Don't forget the Mountain Lion Recovery Partition – use this to reinstall OS X.

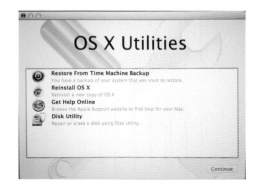

Cannot Eject a Disk or Drive

Sometimes a CD, DVD, or USB drive will not eject. On older Macs, the CD/DVD drive had a small hole where you could push a paperclip and the disk would be ejected but with modern Macs this is no longer an option.

Disk is in use

If you open a document on a CD, DVD, or USB drive with an app and fail to close the document before ejecting the disk you will receive the message:

To eject the disk, close the document or quit the app and then try to eject the disk. Chances are it will eject successfully.

Eject CD or DVD that fails to eject

For a variety of reasons optical disks can simply refuse to eject:

1 Restart the Mac

2 Hold down the eject button as the Mac starts to boot up

The CD/DVD will probably be ejected.

Another solution is to open Disk Utility, click the CD in the left pane, then click Eject or you can open Terminal and type **drutil tray eject**.

Running out of Disk Space

Over time, you install apps, take videos and accumulate large numbers of files that take up the space on your hard drive. Eventually your drive becomes full, or close to full. How can you see what's eating all your space? You could go through your drive manually, folder by folder or you could use an app such as GrandPerspective or OmniDiskSweeper which shows you the largest files on your drive. You can then move or delete these.

GrandPerspective

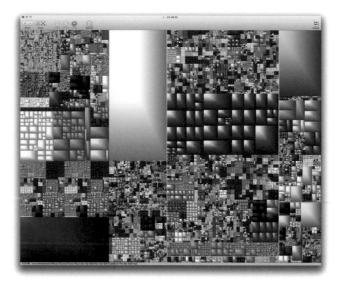

Using GrandPerspective you can see three very large files in the image above. Deleting these would salvage a lot of space on this disk!

OminDiskSweeper

Corrupt Preference Files

Corrupt Preference files can cause major problems when running apps. When you install an app, various files are added to your system, including the Preference file which contains information about your computer and the way you have set up your app. For example, for a word processing app the Preference file contains information about page size, printing preferences, default font and other variables. The app will load the Preference file as it starts up. If the Preference file becomes corrupt over time (not uncommon) the app will misbehave or quit.

If an app starts behaving badly one of the first things you should do is delete its Preference file. The app will then create a new Preference file and your problem may be sorted.

Deleting a Preference file

1 Go to your **~/Library/Preferences** (where ~ is your Home folder)

2 Scroll through the Preferences until you find a file for your app (the file will end with **.plist**)

3 **Trash the file** and restart the app

In the example below I have located the Finder's Preference file which I can drag to the Trash. The Finder will immediately make a new .plist file.

Repair Disks

Over time, computer media such as disks (including USB disks) can become defective, with bad sectors. When you try to read or write data to the drive you start seeing error messages. If a drive ever starts behaving strangely, it is a good idea to check the disk integrity using Disk Utility and to repair the disk if any defects are found. The computer will make a note of the bad sectors on the disk and will not write data to those sectors.

Repairing a drive

1 Open **Disk Utility**

2 Click on the **First Aid** tab, locate your disk from those listed in the pane on the left, and then click **Verify Disk**

3 If an error is found using Verify Disk then click **Repair Disk**

4 If Disk Repair cannot repair the disk you will be advised to backup as many files as you can before reformatting the drive

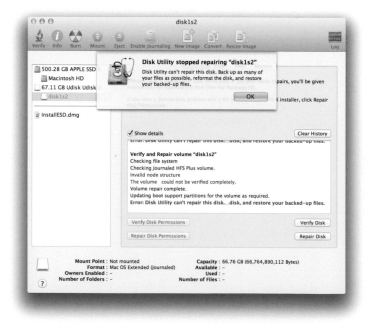

Speed Up your Mac!

Is your Mac starting to feeling sluggish and less responsive than it was when you first got it? Chances are you have items loading at startup that could be disabled, and various other settings that are slowing the whole thing down.

Suggestions for speeding up a slow Mac

- Add more RAM — beef it up to 8 or 12 GB if you can

- Disable unwanted login items

- Defragment the hard drive

- Remove unused System Preferences (the ones added by third party apps)

- Clear caches, temporary files and other junk using OnyX, MainMenu or CCleaner

- Don't run too many apps at once

- Restart your Mac from time to time

- Move massive files to external drives, e.g. large video files. This will free up useful hard drive space, then defragment the drive

Force an App to Close

Sometimes apps hang (become unresponsive) and you get the endless spinning beachball, or when you try to quit an app it stubbornly refuses to quit no matter how many times you try.

You can take control and force the app to quit using the Force Quit menu option.

Warning: sometimes an app may appear unresponsive (not responding) but is actually in the middle of processing data and if you leave it a little while longer the app behaves normally. Before you quit, make absolutely sure the app is truly unresponsive. Once you quit, the chances are you will lose any unsaved work you may have!

Force Quit an app

1   Go to **Apple Menu > Force Quit...**

2   From the window that opens choose the app you wish to quit, select it by clicking on it then click **Force Quit**

Force Quit Applications

If an application doesn't respond for a while, select its name and click Relaunch.

- Adobe Illustrator CS4
- Cyberduck
- Expression Media
- InDesign
- iTunes
- Mail
- Messages
- Microsoft Entourage
- Microsoft Excel
- Photoshop
- RapidWeaver
- Safari (not responding)
- TextEdit
- **Finder**

You can open this window by pressing Command-Option-Escape.

[Relaunch]

Memory Hogs

Apps use variable amounts of RAM and CPU power to run. Some are lean and use little but others are total memory hogs and can cause your Mac to crawl to a halt making it very difficult to do anything.

The Utility Activity Monitor allows you to see how much CPU and RAM various processes are using. If necessary, you can quit a memory hog directly from Activity Monitor and regain control of your Mac. Video apps, animation software, virtualization apps such as Parallels and VMWare use a fair bit of power in order to run. When these apps are busy they can make your Mac slow to a crawl, especially if you have limited RAM or if the Mac is old.

Using Activity Monitor

1 Go to **Utilities > Activity Monitor** and launch the app

2 Using the drop-down menu at the top right select All Processes, My Processes, etc to view the running apps and see if any are using huge amounts of your Mac's processor

3 You can select an app and click **Quit** if you want to quit the app

PID	Process Name	User	% CPU ▼	Threads	Real Mem	Kind	Virtual Mem
17147	prl_vm_app	drewprovan2	28.3	33	1.08 GB	Intel (64 bit)	1.19 GB
1843	Dictate	drewprovan2	4.6	16	368.6 MB	Intel	406.7 MB
577	InDesign	drewprovan2	2.9	27	748.3 MB	Intel	719.5 MB
17133	Parallels Desktop	drewprovan2	2.4	19	187.1 MB	Intel (64 bit)	126.4 MB
937	iTunes	drewprovan2	1.8	32	420.1 MB	Intel (64 bit)	651.1 MB
17112	Activity Monitor	drewprovan2	1.4	2	34.7 MB	Intel (64 bit)	47.3 MB
727	Photoshop	drewprovan2	0.8	21	1.05 GB	Intel	1.13 GB
16810	Flash Player (Safari Internet plu...	drewprovan2	0.7	12	45.4 MB	Intel (64 bit)	116.2 MB
16904	iPhoto	drewprovan2	0.6	48	321.5 MB	Intel	310.3 MB
825	Expression Media	drewprovan2	0.2	25	56.9 MB	Intel	64.3 MB
406	Little Snitch Network Monitor	drewprovan2	0.2	4	6.9 MB	Intel	51.4 MB
356	SystemUIServer	drewprovan2	0.0	4	50.2 MB	Intel (64 bit)	49.8 MB
420	WePrint Server	drewprovan2	0.0	10	86.3 MB	Intel	111.0 MB
425	Dropbox	drewprovan2	0.0	17	49.4 MB	Intel	68.3 MB
357	Finder	drewprovan2	0.0	13	89.4 MB	Intel (64 bit)	241.3 MB
17183	mdworker	drewprovan2	0.0	3	8.1 MB	Intel (64 bit)	42.9 MB
9793	GrandPerspective	drewprovan2	0.0	8	162.0 MB	Intel	200.9 MB

In this example *prl_vm_app* (Parallels Desktop virtualization app) is using a fair bit of my Mac's power (28.3%).

Wireless Problem Solving

Some Macs running Mountain Lion drop their Wi-Fi connections randomly. On occasions the Mac reconnects automatically but other times it fails.

Add a new network

1 Go to **System Preferences > Network**

2 Pull down the **Location** menu and choose **Edit Locations...**

3 Click the **+** button to add a new location and give it whatever name you want

4 Click **Done**

5 On the Network screen click **Network Name** and join the wireless network

Now renew the DHCP lease

1 From the Network panel click **Advanced** (lower right corner) then click the TCP/IP tab

2 Ensure Configure IPv4 is set to **Using DHCP** then click **Renew DHCP Lease** then click **Apply**

3 The Mac should remember the network better!

14 Miscellaneous Tips

In this section we will look at some window tricks, AirPlay mirroring your Mac, and other tweaks you can make. We will also explore the numerous Accessibility options.

Window Tricks

Close a Finder window while you open an app

This is not exactly a killer tip but it is useful nonetheless. Quite often if you have multiple windows open, including Applications or Utilities, and you double-click an app the Applications window remains open:

- Hold down **Option** *then* **double-click** the app and the window (e.g. Applications) will close

Close all open Finder windows in one go!

If you have lots of Finder windows across your desktop you can close them by clicking one at a time or you can close them all at the same time:

- Hold down **Option** then click the **Close** button and all the windows will disappear at once!

Resize your icons in Finder windows

I like my icons really small but sometimes it's great to have huge icons:

 Open a Finder window and change to **Icon View** (⌘ + 1)

 Use the slider at the bottom right and slide to the right to make the icons large

AirPlay Mirroring

This allows you to display your Mac's screen on a TV hooked up to Apple TV. The "Air" part is there because the mirroring is wireless. Both Mac and Apple TV must be on the same network so they can see each other.

AirPlay mirroring is very easy to set up, as you will see from the instructions below.

To use AirPlay Mirroring

1. Your TV must be connected to Apple TV 2 or later

2. Your Mac must be on the same Wi-Fi network as the Apple TV

3. Switch on the TV and Apple TV and make sure you can see the Apple TV menu on the screen

4. From your Mac go to **System Preferences > Displays > AirPlay mirroring: OFF/ON**

5. Choose the **Apple TV** for mirroring

You should then see the Mac screen displayed on your TV.

Creating Digital Signatures

A digital signature is useful if you need to email a PDF of a letter. You can also use it in Apple Mail signatures so a personalized handwritten signature is appended to your emails.

Getting the best scanned image

1 **Use a thick black marker pen** and write your signature (fairly large size) on white paper

2 **Scan the image** at high resolution using your scanner

3 Take into **Preview** or **Photoshop** and crop so that there is not too much redundant white space

4 **Whiten the image** slightly to avoid having a gray rectangle around your signature when dropped into, e.g. a Microsoft Word document

Example of digital signature (TIFF) file

Digital signature dropped onto a Pages document.

Apps for Tweaking your Mac

There are several great apps allowing you to make changes to the look and feel of your Mac. These have been touched upon earlier in the book but we will look at the main contenders here: OnyX, Cocktail, TinkerTool and Mountain Tweaks. (Mountain Tweaks is covered on Page 57.)

OnyX

Provides a large suite of maintenance and tweaking tools.

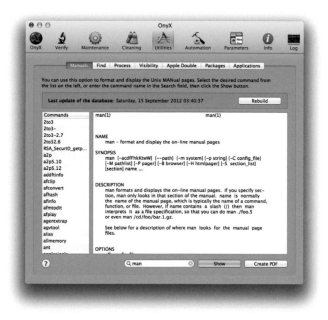

Cocktail

Probably the best suite, with a huge number of tweaks and maintenance tools.

TinkerTool

Useful, with similar functions to most of the others. Provides useful information about the system, drives, etc.

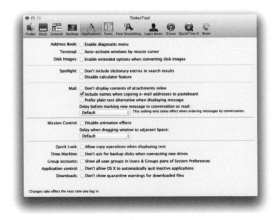

Optimizing Accessibility

Apple has always been very proactive in designing its hardware and software for use by people with visual and hearing impairment, and other disabilities.

Invert screen

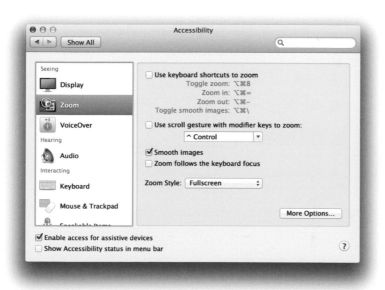

Zoom

...cont'd

Speakable items

Keyboard

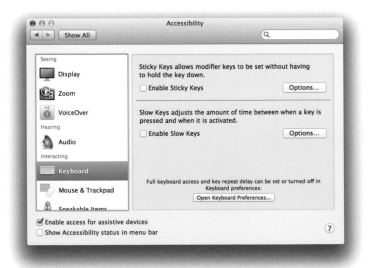

Index

T

U

V